THE
MAKING
OF A SLUM

Other Books by
Michael Dorman

WE SHALL OVERCOME

THE SECOND MAN
The Changing Role
of the Vice Presidency

THE KING OF THE COURTROOM

SECRET SERVICE STORY

UNDER 21
A Young People's Guide
to Legal Rights

PAYOFF
The Role of Organized Crime
in American Politics

THE MAKING OF A SLUM

Michael Dorman

 DELACORTE PRESS / NEW YORK

Library of Congress Cataloging in Publication Data
Dorman, Michael.
    The making of a slum.
    1. Hunts Point, New York.   2. Slums—New York (City)
I. Title
HN80.H9D67   301.36'3'09747275   72–3442

Designed by Julian Hamer

To the memory of my grandparents
Hunts Pointers all,
and to William Bradford Huie,
an Alabamian who taught me
reverence for my roots.

1

Hazel Fleming is past the age of sixty. She has classic American beauty, an unlined face, a lantern jaw, and an Irish temper. She also has a stoic determination and a philosophy. At the moment, her philosophy is put firmly and simply: "Damn it, this is my home. I was born here and I'm gonna die here. *They* are not gonna drive *me* out!"

Hazel Fleming is not a character in a Western movie, bent on driving off marauding Indians or claim-jumpers. She is a real human being, born and bred in a section of New York City known as Hunts Point. Once, not long ago, Hunts Point was a garden spot of pleasant middle-class homes with verdant back yards—a pastoral setting where people of many national origins and religions lived together in tranquillity. Unlikely as it seems, this island of relative greenery amid the concrete canyons of the Bronx even featured a few cows and a herd of goats within recent years. Today, however, Hunts Point is perhaps the worst urban jungle in the United States— teeming with filth, misery, narcotics addicts, thieves, looters, and killers.

When Hazel Fleming says *"they"* are not going to drive her out, she refers to the hordes of lawless marauders who have descended on Hunts Point as thousands of destitute families, mostly black or Puerto Rican, have displaced families that had lived there for generations. Miss Fleming is one of the few old-timers who remains, but she pays a price for her stubborn determination. Within one year, she has been slugged and robbed three times while walking the three blocks from the subway station to her home. Her three-story brick house has been burglarized by thieves who simply battered their way through a wall in broad daylight to gain entry—fully confident that, even if they were seen, nobody would call the police. She has seen automobiles parked on her street stripped of wheels, motors, and other parts while policemen stood by and watched.

It is not the waves of desperate poor people now living in squalor in her neighborhood whom Miss Fleming condemns; she recognizes that most of them, with her, are victims of the same criminal element. What she condemns is the system of governmental neglect and citizen apathy that has allowed her beloved Hunts Point to be transformed into a ghastly ghetto within the past two decades.

The magnitude of Hunts Point's decay is almost beyond description. As the *New York Times* put it after examining this decay in detail: "In basic ways, portions of the Hunts Point section of the southeast Bronx have ceased to be a part of New York City. Many city services, such as police protection, garbage collection, water supply—and citizen obligations, such as payment of taxes, decent maintenance of property, some semblance of civil order—do not occur with any degree of predictability in Hunts Point. Repeated visits to Hunts Point uncover so much that is not supposed to be America that the visitor wonders if he has suddenly entered a time machine and been transported back to frontier days. Nearly everything seems touched by lawlessness."

In one part of Hunts Point, a study has shown that residents have less than one chance in twenty of dying a natural death. The study was made by Dr. Michael Baden, a New York City associate medical examiner, based on the actual

[2]

deaths that occurred in this section during a period of several months. Of the thirty-seven deaths, only two were of natural causes. That figure is all the more astounding when it is compared with the statistic that just seven percent of all the deaths in New York City are of unnatural causes. Of the thirty-five unnatural deaths examined by Dr. Baden, five were murders —including the strangling of a seventy-five-year-old widow, three fatal stabbings, and one fatal shooting. Seven persons, ranging from a sixteen-year-old Negro to a thirty-year-old Puerto Rican, died after injecting heroin into their veins. Eleven died of alcoholism, the youngest a thirty-year-old Puerto Rican. One man died after he got drunk and fell down a flight of stairs. Four children died in falls from windows—a number whose significance stands out when it is noted that only sixteen children fell from windows during this period in all of New York City. Three other children were battered to death by their parents. The remainder of the victims suffered from an assortment of other acts of violence.

Such violence is so commonplace in Hunts Point that children scarcely pause in their street games while gun battles rage about them. Adults gaze calmly from the grimy windows of their tenements while robberies, stabbings, and shootings occur on the streets below. Often they do not even bother to call the police. St. Athanasius Catholic Church, which serves Hunts Point, has had to abandon using a poor box. The box was stolen so many times that the priests finally gave up.

Law-abiding residents of Hunts Point live in a constant state of siege—their windows barred and doors secured with as many as half a dozen locks to protect them against junkie thieves. Addicts steal even the plumbing pipes out of occupied buildings, to sell to scrap-metal dealers, and often leave raging floods behind as they make their getaways. Landlords must hire off-duty policemen to guard them on days when they make rent collections and carry them to banks. One apartment-house landlord whose tenants were terrorized by thugs hired as his building superintendent a convicted murderer who patrols the halls with a machete, an ax, and a 160-pound German shepherd attack dog.

In many buildings, residents somehow survive for months without water, heat, or electricity. Landlords simply walk off and abandon their buildings in despair. The city government then takes over the buildings, declares them unfit for human habitation, and yet permits tenants to stay on with token rents of a dollar a month. Children sleep three and four to a bed while rats and roaches scurry around them. Heroin is peddled everywhere, and used by children as young as six. As one Puerto Rican mother puts it: "We don't care about marijuana here. If our kids just take marijuana, we consider ourselves lucky."

How did all this happen? How, in just twenty years or so, did Hunts Point rot so decisively? Other sections of major American cities have witnessed the flight of white middle-class residents and the concurrent influx of poor members of minority groups. In many cases, it is true, the quality of life in these neighborhoods has declined sharply. But probably nowhere has a neighborhood sunk to such depths so quickly as in Hunts Point. Barry Schweid, who grew up in Hunts Point and now serves as the Associated Press correspondent at the United States Supreme Court, puts it this way: "The name 'Hunts Point' has become a pejorative. People use it as synonymous with everything that's filthy, degraded, and hopeless—the way they used to use the words 'Black Hole of Calcutta.'"

In short, Hunts Point represents in microcosm all that is wrong with decaying American cities today. If the causes of Hunts Point's blight can be discovered, and if possible remedies can be suggested, the implications will stretch far beyond the boundaries of one neighborhood, one city, or one state. If Hunts Point can be saved, there will be hope for countless other ghettos. If Hunts Point is doomed, one can only despair for the entire American society.

This book seeks to explore what has happened in Hunts Point, how it has happened, why it has happened, and what may happen in the future. It is written in the hope that it may point to a day when the name "Hunts Point" will no longer be a pejorative but rather a living testament to America's capacity for regeneration—not alone of buildings but of people, not alone of material comforts but of the human spirit itself.

2

Mrs. Kathleen Wiener, who now spends her winters in Miami and her summers in an apartment on Manhattan's West End Avenue, recalls moving to Hunts Point as a child of five in 1908. Her family had previously lived in upper Manhattan. The move to Hunts Point, then considered virtually "out in the country," was evidence of the family's upward mobility. "It took us almost a day to make the trip from Manhattan to the wilds of Hunts Point in a horse-drawn carriage," Mrs. Wiener remembers.

The family's new home was to be in a three-story, two-family brick house on Irvine Street—one block east of the area's main drag, Hunts Point Avenue. There were about ten two-family houses on the street, all built by one of Mrs. Wiener's uncles. "When we finally arrived, the gutter was a sea of mud," she recalls. "The carriage driver and another man gathered planks and put them under the wheels so the carriage wouldn't get bogged down."

The surrounding area was dotted with farms. When Mrs. Wiener and her family got settled and her grandmother planted a vegetable garden in the spacious back yard, there was a constant battle to keep the goats from neighboring farms from destroying the crops. "There was also a bull a few blocks away that was always giving us a fright by chasing us,"

Mrs. Wiener says. A few blocks east of Irvine Street was the Bronx River, then a pure fresh-water artery but now a polluted, junk-strewn creek. To the south, at the lower end of Hunts Point Avenue, lay the East River.

Growing up in Hunts Point in those days was idyllic—an existence that makes it all the more incredible for Mrs. Wiener to contemplate the horror of a Hunts Point childhood today. "In summer evenings, we gathered on the stoop of one of the houses and sang and played quiet talk games," she recalls. "During school vacations, we played Red Rover and hide-and-seek, or jumped rope. There were summer picnics and June Walks every year, and just about all the kids took part. We all wore costumes for the June Walks—usually the same ones, year after year. I remember mine well. I was always Miss Liberty, since I had red hair and blue eyes, which fitted in with the American flag color-scheme. I guess my freckles could have passed for the stars."

Today, for many of the children in Hunts Point, such sparetime pursuits as those described by Mrs. Wiener are unthinkable. When not in school, these children spend much of their time stealing. Many must steal to support drug habits. Others steal because it is the thing to do to prove themselves to their friends. "I been stealin' since I was eight," says Hector Torres, now all of twelve, who lives in an apartment house a half-block away from Mrs. Wiener's childhood home. "I steal parts from cars or sometimes I sneak into a store and swipe somethin'." He sells his loot to a fence, and uses the proceeds to buy marijuana. "I don't use 'H' [heroin]," he says. "I ain't stupid. But there's nothin' wrong with smokin' pot." Hector has been picked up by the police several times, but released without being taken to court.

During her youth, Mrs. Wiener recalls, perhaps the outstanding characteristic of Hunts Point children was their discipline. "I remember, during an epidemic of polio, no child was allowed even to cross the street to see a friend," she says.

"The only contact we had with each other was to shout from house to house. I don't remember any one of us who even thought of disobeying the rule."

Today, with rare exceptions, such discipline is unheard of among Hunts Point children. Youngsters of eight and nine can be seen wandering the streets alone as late as two A.M. Truancy is rampant. Street gangs armed with such weapons as zip guns and switchblade knives fight viciously to protect their turfs against invasion by rivals from other neighborhoods.

After Mrs. Wiener had lived at Hunts Point for several years, trolley-car service was inaugurated along Hunts Point Avenue—connecting with lines that served other sections of the Bronx. Housewives who previously had walked a mile or more on shopping excursions to stores on Southern Boulevard and Westchester Avenue were treated to the luxury of hauling their bundles home on the trolleys. "Often, a housewife would forget one or two items on her shopping list," Mrs. Wiener says. "Since we all knew the trolley schedules by heart, the housewife would wait for the trolley to come by and hand the motorman a list of her missing items. When he got up to the shopping district, he'd slip into one of the stores and buy what she'd forgotten. She'd be waiting to pick it up and pay the motorman the next time he came by her stop."

The trolleys are now long gone from Hunts Point, replaced by buses, whose drivers work in constant terror of holdup men and other thugs. Many taxi drivers, fearing for their lives, refuse to take passengers to and from Hunts Point. Grocery wholesalers similarly refuse to send delivery trucks into the area; shopkeepers must drive to the wholesalers' supply depots to pick up their merchandise.

During Mrs. Wiener's childhood, she recalls, "one of the delights of the neighborhood" was a firehouse a block from her home—at the corner of Seneca Avenue and Faile Street. To her child's eye, the sight of horses galloping down the street with a fire-wagon in tow was the height of adventure.

"If a cooking pot or stove started burning or even smoking badly, one of us would run to the firehouse and the firemen would trot over with a hose and put it out," Mrs. Wiener says. "We knew them all by their first names and they certainly knew ours."

Today, that same firehouse still stands at the corner of Seneca Avenue and Faile Street. But the relationship between the firemen and the citizenry has changed radically over the years. As in many ghetto areas of New York and other large cities, residents coexist in a state of hostility with such public servants as firemen. They complain that the fire protection they get is haphazard, indifferent, and sometimes nonexistent. They often show their anger by turning in false alarms and then pelting the firemen with rocks and bottles as the fire engines race through the streets.

The Hunts Point described by Mrs. Wiener, as she knew it during the first and second decades of the twentieth century, did not change very much in the following three decades. Some of the farms disappeared, to be sure, and were replaced by apartment houses rising all of seven or eight stories. Horse-drawn wagons were replaced by automobiles, trolleys by buses. But the pleasant, well-tended two-family and three-family homes, their back yards filled with flower gardens and fruit trees, remained. And, more important, many of the old families remained. For a section of New York, a city where residents had a high degree of transiency, Hunts Point was a remarkably stable community. In many ways, it resembled a small town more than a part of a metropolis. Children born there tended to grow up there, fall in love with neighborhood sweethearts, marry, and stay there. The few who did move away often left relatives behind, and thus kept their ties with the old neighborhood.

For many years, Hunts Point was a melting pot. Jews of German and Eastern European descent lived side by side with Irish, Italian, and Polish Catholics and Anglo-Saxon Protestants. On Irvine Street, where Mrs. Wiener grew up, the residents shortly after the turn of the century bore such names as Jaretski, Santini, Padernak, Lowy, Cowen, Spieler, Matuszeski, Engelman, Sunshine, Russo, Bennett, Frey, and Goldberg. By the late 1940's, members of many of those families were still there. Those who had left had been succeeded by families bearing such names as Sullivan (Irish Catholic); Wolf, Scheidlinger, and Saidel (Russian and German Jews); Fetcho (Czech Catholic); Murray (Scottish Protestant); and Van Dientz (Dutch Catholic). During the forties, the first Latin-American family moved into Irvine Street. The family, named Ramirez, was of Cuban descent and owned a small business in the neighborhood that produced fine, hand-rolled cigars from Cuban tobacco. A short time after the arrival of the Ramirezes, a Negro family named Adams moved into the adjoining street—Seneca Avenue. If the older residents felt any resentment toward the Ramirezes or the Adamses, they didn't show it. Both families were welcomed warmly and accepted fully into the life of the community.

Today, only a scattered few members of the old families remain on Irvine Street. They find themselves surrounded by Latin-Americans, mostly Puerto Ricans, and Negroes. Names such as Ruiz, Gonzales, Mendoza, Torres, and Contreras have replaced those such as Sullivan and Saidel. But the tranquillity of past years, characterized by acceptance of divergent ethnic backgrounds, is gone. Hunts Point today is seething with tensions based in no small measure on racial and ethnic prejudice. Members of the few remaining old families, who were willing to welcome a few Latin and Negro families during the forties, now find themselves enraged by the mass influx. They make no secret of their deep resentment over what they consider the "takeover" of their neighborhood by hordes of dark-skinned newcomers. Many of the newcomers, in turn, detest the remaining white families, accusing them of long-time exploitation and oppression of minority groups.

The Latins and blacks, meanwhile, are constantly at each other's throats. Negroes brand their Spanish-American neighbors "spics" and are called "niggers" in return, often leading knives to flash and guns to blast in senseless outbursts of racial violence.

"These people [Negroes and Latins] are animals," says one old-time resident, Samuel Aronow. "Look at the way they live—like pigs. They throw their garbage out the windows. They never wash. They let their children run wild at all hours of the night. They don't work. Why should they? They get welfare money for sitting home on their asses. Animals, that's all they are. I wish I could move away from here, but I can't afford it. I'm retired, and I own my house—but I couldn't get anything for it if I sold it. So I'm stuck here for the rest of my life—living with these animals."

Joseph Nelson, a Negro who has lived in Hunts Point since 1969, sees things differently. "These white people have had everything their way for so long—" he says. "They been holdin' us down. You think we like livin' in these shit-houses? Just the other day my daughter—she's two years old—she got bit by a rat that must've been a foot long. Who do you think owns these buildings? The whites do. They don't take care of 'em. They don't do anything about the rats or the roaches or the filth. All they want is our money. I pay eighty-five dollars a month for four rooms. There's no hot water. In the winter, there's no heat. The landlord won't fix anything. We call the city to report him, but nothin' happens. White people say we live like trash—and maybe we do—but they drive us to it."

Armando Guitterez, who left his native Puerto Rico for New York in 1958, and moved to Hunts Point from Harlem in 1967, says: "If I could afford to live anywhere else, I'd move today. I'm twenty-nine years old, and I got five kids. I hate it here and I hate having my kids grow up here. A few weeks ago, some nigger kids beat up my oldest boy. He came home with his head and his face bleeding. He hadn't done a damn thing to them; they beat the hell out of him just because he wasn't black. He's seven years old. Can you picture something like that? Ah, what the hell can you do?"

One of the most discouraging aspects of life in Hunts Point today is that there are multitudinous forces driving the residents apart and few counterbalancing forces bringing them together to improve their common lot. A sense of community pride and identity, once an essential ingredient of Hunts Point life, is now almost totally absent. In the past, this community spirit was rarely articulated, but it was very much present and made itself felt in a variety of ways.

When World War II ended in 1945, for example, residents on virtually every street in Hunts Point voluntarily banded together to toss "block parties" welcoming home discharged GI's. Each family chipped in a few dollars for the purchase of beer and soft drinks and the rental of loudspeakers to pipe recorded music into the streets. Festive decorations were strung from windows and utility poles. Housewives spent weeks cooking their favorite delicacies. On the day of a block party, police arranged to close the street to traffic. Tables laden with food and drink were set up on the sidewalks during the late afternoon; gutters were kept clear for dancing. Often the parties lasted through most of the night, with celebrants dancing in the streets until three or four A.M. For New York City—with its reputation as an indifferent, cold-hearted metropolis—such goings-on may have seemed strangely out of place. But they were not so for Hunts Point in those days.

"Something like that would be impossible around here today," says Harry Ferguson, who has lived in Hunts Point for more than thirty years. "For one thing, the people here now—the law-abiding ones, anyway—are afraid to go out on the streets after dark. Besides, you couldn't get the people in the neighborhood to join together to do anything. Most of them hardly know each other. They're so frightened they stay home, with the doors and windows locked, a good part of the time. People move in and move out all the time without anyone even noticing. In the old days, it was a big event when someone new moved into the neighborhood. Everybody would visit the new people and make them feel welcome; the wives would take them pies and that kind of thing. Nowadays, I don't know half the people who live a few doors from me."

This lack of neighborliness makes itself felt in many ways. In former years, many Orthodox Jews in Hunts Point—in keeping with their religious tenets—refrained from turning on their electricity or gas on the Sabbath. Often, Gentile neighbors would either visit the Jewish homes to turn on the utilities or, in some cases, even invite their Jewish neighbors to eat with them on the Sabbath (going to the trouble of buying only kosher foods for those meals and observing Jewish dietary laws). "There's none of that any more," says Mrs. Ida Rubin, an Orthodox Jewish widow. "There's nobody around here I would trust to come into my home. I've had to start violating some of the Sabbath customs. It nearly kills me, but I've got no choice."

Also missing from Hunts Point today are many of the organizations that once helped forge a community identity— Boy Scout and Girl Scout troops, adult social clubs, civic and religious groups. For many years, one of the greatest sources of pride in the neighborhood was Boy Scout Troop 186. No ordinary troop, 186 had won a national reputation for its wide range of activities and the intense dedication of its members. It had an alumni association with scores of members who remained active although their Scouting days had ended officially twenty or thirty years earlier.

The troop's chief claim to fame was that it was one of the few Scout organizations in the country to specialize in emergency-service projects. Its members were trained to carry out rescue missions, using thousands of dollars' worth of equipment owned by the troop, and to help policemen and firemen at disaster scenes. The troop's equipment included a pair of two-wheeled trailers that could be pulled through the streets by the Scouts or hitched to automobiles and towed. Inside the trailers were wooden cases filled with rescue gear, first-aid supplies, emergency cooking equipment, and the like. One of the trailers was designed so that it could be quickly rigged with a rescue derrick capable of lifting thousands of pounds. If a disaster victim were trapped under piles of debris, for example, the derrick could be used to free him. It could also be equipped with a wire-basket stretcher to lift accident victims from inaccessible places. In addition, a slight conversion enabled the Scouts to use the derrick as a breeches buoy, to perform such tasks as rescuing a fire victim from a window several stories above the street. The second trailer could be dismantled to form a field kitchen for feeding disaster victims. Cooking and serving equipment carried in the trailer enabled the Scouts to feed several hundred persons in emergencies.

Although few occasions arose when the Scouts and their equipment were actually pressed into emergency-service duty, the boys considered themselves on virtually constant alert status. They maintained a mobilization system designed to bring all members of the troop rushing from their homes to a central point in case of a crisis. And every Saturday they spent several hours practicing their rescue operations. For the practice sessions, they pulled the trailers through the streets from a garage rented by the troop on Garrison Avenue to the curbside of a two-family house at 822 Manida Street owned by the Scoutmaster, Bernard Heineman. The leadership of Troop 186 had been a Heineman family tradition. Bernard Heineman's father, Joseph, had been the troop's first Scoutmaster. He had been succeeded by Bernard's brother, Bert, and then by Bernard.

In front of the Heineman home, the Scouts ran endlessly through their drills—racing against a stopwatch held by the Scoutmaster. The all-time troop record for unloading both trailers, erecting a derrick on one and converting the other into a field kitchen, was four minutes flat. It had been set during the 1930's. Try as they might, the Scouts of the forties and early fifties could never match it—but they never gave up the effort. Neighborhood residents, although occasionally annoyed by the noise and inconvenience the Scouts and their equipment created in the streets, generally took a measure of pride in the troop's constructive activities.

This pride was enhanced by the national attention given the troop. Numerous national television shows featured segments in which the Scouts demonstrated their rescue techniques. The boys also became regular fixtures in major New York parades, carrying out rescue exercises while rolling down Fifth Avenue in their trailers. When national Boy Scout officials decided to create a new badge honoring Scouts involved in emergency-service work, the first such insignia awarded anywhere in the country was presented to a member of Troop 186 by sportscaster Mel Allen at a national meeting in the Waldorf-Astoria Hotel.

The troop was even capable of performing water-borne rescue missions. It had a Sea Scout unit that owned a large sailboat moored at City Island, a nautical section of the Bronx. While the boat was sailed primarily for pleasure, it was available for emergency duty if needed.

However, all the tradition and spirit of service connected with Troop 186 could not keep the troop alive when Hunts Point underwent its traumatic change of character. Most of the Negro and Latin-American boys whose families moved into the area seemed to show little or no interest in Scouting. As one current Hunts Point youth, thirteen-year-old Arturo Gotay, put it: "Me be a Boy Scout? You kiddin'? That's for queers. My buddies would laugh like hell at me." Troop 186 eventually withered and died. Regional Boy Scout officials launched a campaign to revive interest in Scouting in Hunts Point, but had little success.

Another element that long played an important role in establishing a sense of community in Hunts Point was sports. Virtually every block in the area had its own stickball team, and a stiff rivalry existed for the neighborhood championship. Stickball, a city game virtually unknown in rural areas, has several variations—all akin to baseball. It is played in the streets with a rubber ball, usually known in New York as a "Spall-deen" because the original models were made by the Spalding Company, and with a broom handle used as a bat. In some versions, the game corresponds almost identically to baseball except for the equipment. There are nine players on each side. The pitcher delivers the ball to home plate on the fly or, in one variation of the game, on a single bounce. The Hunts Point version of stickball, however, was played without a pitcher or catcher. There were seven players to a side. The batter either hit the ball fungo-style or threw it into the air and hit it on a bounce. It is a bit of New York folklore that stickball players are rated according to how many "sewers" they can hit. A "sewer" is the distance between one manhole cover in the street and another. If a stickball player is called a "two-sewer hitter," he's considered pretty fair. If he can hit "three sewers," he's a slugger.

At Hunts Point in the 1940's, most of the three-sewer hitters in their early teens played on a team called the Hawks. Once a boy had established himself as a star on one of the lesser teams in the neighborhood—such as the Americans of Irvine Street or the Eagles of Bryant Avenue—he might be honored with an invitation to step up to faster company and join the Hawks. It was the stickball equivalent of being called up from Triple-A baseball to the major leagues. The Hawks not only represented the cream of Hunts Point's stickball crop; they also took on all comers from other sections of New York.

A short, tubby youth named Larry Moskowitz was the perennial captain of the Hawks, and ruled the team with indisputable authority. Moskowitz, called "Mosky" by his team-

[16]

mates, had once read a biography of the tyrannical New York Giant manager, John McGraw, and it had apparently gone to his head. He was determined to be even more iron-fisted with his players than McGraw. Any Hawk player caught smoking, staying out late, or otherwise "breaking training" was subject to instant punishment by Mosky—punishment that could be as severe as expulsion from the team. Some of the players, mindful that John McGraw had been known as "Little Napoleon," referred to Mosky as "Fat Napoleon"—but never to his face. Mosky's captaincy of the team of all-stars was puzzling, since he was far from an outstanding stickball player. In the words of Ring Lardner, "Although he was a bad fielder, he was also a very poor hitter." Besides that, he was a very slow base-runner. But he claimed to know a lot of "inside stuff" about the intricacies of stickball, so nobody challenged his right to install himself permanently as the team's third baseman.

After serving apprenticeships in stickball, the better Hunts Point athletes usually moved on to baseball. Some of the best of the lot made it to a fast semi-pro team called the Hunts Point Cardinals, which played its home games at a small stadium off Hunts Point Avenue named Kelton Oval. The Cardinals, whose uniforms duplicated those worn by the St. Louis Cardinals, played against some of the best semi-pro teams in the East. They had a loyal following of fans, whose enthusiasm was even greater for the Cardinals than for that other Bronx team, the New York Yankees. The ball team served as a positive force in welding a community identity in Hunts Point. When the Cardinals won a game, the entire neighborhood could share in the triumph. When the team lost, the gloom might not quite have matched that in Mudville after the mighty Casey had struck out; but it did not rank far behind. Many Hunts Point athletes anxious to retain their amateur standing played their baseball for the high school that served the area, James Monroe. For years, Monroe turned out some of the country's leading baseball prospects. Among the school's alumni who went on to the major leagues were Detroit Tiger slugger Hank Greenberg, San Francisco Giant manager Charlie Fox, and New York Met first baseman Ed Kranepool.

Hunts Point was also noted as a breeding ground for basketball players. Every school yard and playground in the neighborhood was filled on afternoons and weekends with kids scrambling to learn the rugged, fast-paced brand of basketball for which New York was renowned. Dozens of teenage club teams competed in annual tournaments conducted at night in community centers operated in the local schools. The better teams went on to compete in citywide tournaments sponsored by the New York City Department of Parks, which led up to championship games at Madison Square Garden. When a Hunts Point team survived the elimination rounds of such a tournament, the entire neighborhood got caught up in the excitement—much the same way a small town in Indiana might if its high school team were in the running for the state championship.

Many Hunts Point kids learned their basketball from a remarkable man named Abe Berkowitz, who served for several decades as the supervisor of a city playground at Faile Street and Spofford Avenue. "Berk," as he was known to thousands of youngsters over the years, showed infinite patience with the neighborhood's fledgling athletes. He spent even more time coaching those with limited ability than he did the potential stars. All year round, no matter how severe the weather, Berk could be found at the playground—usually in khaki slacks and a tattered sweatshirt—ready to provide pointers to anyone who was interested. As he grew older, he gradually began losing his eyesight. But he never complained or discussed his problems with his young protégés. He just continued going about his coaching duties until, one melancholy day, he was forced to retire.

Among the basketball players who first learned the game from Berk were identical twin brothers named Dick and Bill Kor. During the 1940's, they formed a sensational backcourt combination in playground, community center, and high school competition. Dick went on to play for New York University during the golden era of New York college basketball. Throughout his college career, thousands of Hunts Pointers huddled around television and radio sets to follow his exploits. Every time he scored, cheers resounded through the neighborhood. During one National Invitation Tournament at Madison Square Garden, Kor came off the bench with seconds to play and sank a basket that gave NYU a one-point victory. Immediately afterward, cheering Hunts Pointers left their TV and radio sets and rushed into the streets to celebrate the "hometown boy's" success. When Kor returned home, he was greeted as a conquering hero. A short time later, he and his neighbors savored the triumph anew when sportscaster Bill Stern reenacted the dramatic last moments of the game—complete with Kor begging NYU Coach Howard Cann to insert him in the lineup—on a national radio show. To many Hunts Pointers, that game-winning basket belonged not only to Kor and NYU; it belonged to the neighborhood and to every kid who had ever dribbled for a layup shot at Berk Berkowitz's playground.

In Hunts Point today, however, sports play hardly any role in the life of the community. There is an occasional stickball game in the streets or a pickup basketball game in a playground or school yard. But there are no organized teams, no Hawks or Cardinals, no focus around which the residents can center their rooting interests. This lack is puzzling in view of the fact that ghetto neighborhoods have traditionally produced many athletes who have found sports to be their chief hope of escape from poverty. Harlem, for example, has long been and continues to be a fertile ground for the breeding of some of the nation's leading basketball prospects.

Why not Hunts Point? Conditions there apparently have deteriorated so badly—so much more so than even a ghetto such as Harlem—that any resemblance to typical American life has almost totally disappeared. And sports, an integral and representative part of that typical life, have gone by the boards along with numerous other American institutions absent in Hunts Point.

As one fourteen-year-old Hunts Point boy put it: "Listen, man, I got a fifty-buck-a-day heroin habit to support. Most of the other guys around here are hooked, too. We got to steal somethin' every day—maybe a coupla times a day—to get the bread to buy junk. Where the hell are we gonna get the time to play basketball? You kiddin' me?"

One of his young companions, hearing this, chimed in: "The game we're playin' is called 'survival.' And there ain't any bigger game than that!"

3

Sherry Leids is a tall, attractive, forty-year-old redhead who teaches emotionally disturbed children. Her husband, Hank, a distinguished, bearded man ten years her senior, is chairman of the science department at a junior high school. They live with their two daughters and a cat in a comfortable house worth about $35,000 in Huntington Township, Long Island. They own a small pleasure boat, which Hank skippers on frequent excursions into Long Island Sound or the Atlantic Ocean. In his remaining spare time, he tinkers with rebuilding a 1938 Pontiac that he keeps in his back yard. All in all, Sherry and Hank seem to be living a close approximation of "the good life." But, both concede, there is something missing. That something is a state of mind, a feeling of kinship with their neighbors, that both knew only during one period of their lives—when they were growing up in Hunts Point.

"There was a kind of closeness—of community—in Hunts Point that I've never felt anywhere else," Sherry says. "There was a warmth I'll never experience anywhere else in my lifetime. My children will never experience it. And that's very sad."

In the housing development in which Hank and Sherry now live, the trappings of upper-middle-class suburbia abound.

There are swimming pools in the back yards, lush sodded lawns, thousands of dollars' worth of shrubbery. Teen-agers have their own cars. Younger children are sent to day camps or sleep-away camps during summer vacations. "But I can't help feeling we and our kids are being deprived of something very important," Sherry says. "There's no sense of community here. Each family is an island—isolated from everyone else. There's almost no visiting back and forth. People are civil to each other, but that's all—just civil. They don't take any interest in each other. What a difference from Hunts Point!"

Sherry moved to Hunts Point in 1941, when she was nine, with her parents, Sol and Fannie Josephowitz, and her older brother, Joe. They had previously lived in another section of the Bronx. "By Hunts Point standards, we were in the lowest economic group," Sherry recalls. "We lived in a three-room apartment at 875 Longfellow Avenue. That was a five-story apartment house. We lived in Apartment 4-D. In Hunts Point, if you lived in an apartment house, you stood in awe of the people who owned private houses. They were the aristocrats. A mother living in an apartment house who was looking over the guys in the neighborhood as prospective boyfriends for her daughter would say: 'He lives *in a private house!*' It was as if he lived in a castle. The highest thing we could aspire to was to live in a private house."

The apartment occupied by Sherry's family was so small that her parents slept in a hallway. She and her brother shared the only bedroom. Each member of the family was allocated one drawer in a four-drawer bureau—the only drawer space in the entire apartment. "When I got old enough to go out on dates, I could never bring the boys into the apartment with me when we got home," Sherry recalls. "We would have had to climb over my parents, who were sleeping in the hallway."

Her parents were Jewish immigrants who had come to the United States from Rumania during the early 1920's. They had met in New York through a Rumanian-American club.

Her father worked as a fabric-cutter for a hat manufacturer. "I had a very strict European upbringing," she says. "When I was a kid, I wasn't allowed out after dark. My parents had to know exactly where I was all the time. We led very structured lives."

Still, even with such restrictions and her family's low economic standard compared with other Hunts Pointers, Sherry remembers her childhood as idyllic. "There was just this great feeling of togetherness in Hunts Point," she says. "Everyone was genuinely interested in everyone else. There was constant visiting back and forth. And there was tremendous ethnic mixing. In our apartment house, we had people of every conceivable ethnic background—Yugoslavs, Italians, Irish, Russians, Germans, Rumanians, Poles. We got along famously. The apartment house was just like one huge family. We shared each other's joys and sorrows. As I said, there was a warmth and closeness that I've never even heard about anywhere else."

Sherry attended Public School 48 on Spofford Avenue, between Faile and Coster Streets, through the sixth grade. There, she made friends with several girls who lived at the Shield of David Home—an orphanage on Bryant Avenue. "I used to climb over the wall of the Shield of David and sneak in to visit them," she recalls. "I thought it was a marvelous place. All of the girls had their own rooms. The home was big and airy and clean. They had a much higher standard of living than mine. So, even though they were orphans, I envied them."

As a child, Sherry was a dreamer and romantic. "I loved to walk down near The Creek [the Bronx River] all by myself," she says. "There were huge vacant lots down there, and I imagined them to be all sorts of romantic places." Although the area near The Creek was often deserted, she never felt any fear. "There just never seemed to be anything to be afraid of in Hunts Point in those days." She recalls that a mentally retarded man named Danny—who might have been taunted as "the village idiot" elsewhere—was completely safe from physical or verbal molestation as he wandered aimlessly through Hunts Point streets. "Danny was forever walking around the neighborhood, pulling a little wagon full of junk," she says. "In other neighborhoods—or in Hunts Point today —he might have been picked on or beaten up by the kids because he was so helpless. But nobody ever dreamed of hurting him or embarrassing him when we were kids. We all kept an eye on him, to be sure nothing happened to him."

After finishing the sixth grade, Sherry went to Junior High School 60—an all-girls school just outside the Hunts Point area. It was in a neighborhood that experienced a mass influx of Negroes and Latin-Americans years earlier than Hunts Point. "Sixty was considered a tough school in a tough neighborhood," Sherry says. "If you didn't want to get beaten up, you had to pay protection money to the tougher girls. I remember my father once brought a hat home from work so I could give it to one of the tough girls. That was my protection payoff." Attending school in the tough neighborhood made her all the more appreciative of the tranquillity in Hunts Point.

Sherry later went on to James Monroe High School and Hunter College, and is currently doing graduate work at the State University of New York branch in Stony Brook, Long Island. She was nineteen when she met her future husband. But although both lived in Hunts Point, it was not there that they met. Because of the disparity in their ages and the fact that they lived at opposite ends of the Hunts Point area, their paths did not cross until they coincidentally took summer jobs in 1951 at a children's camp in upstate New York. "It was called Camp Navajo and it was near Rhinebeck, New York," Sherry recalls. "I was a counselor and Hank was a supervisor. We didn't have much to do with each other all summer. But I knew he lived somewhere in the Bronx, fairly close to where I did. At the end of the summer, I asked him to give me a ride home from the camp, and that's when we learned we both lived in Hunts Point. One thing led to another, we started dating, and we got married in 1953."

Hank Leids was among the "aristocratic" Hunts Pointers living in private houses, who were envied by apartment-dwellers. "It was a two-story house at 634 Coster Street, between Randall and Spofford Avenues, right near P.S. 48," Hank says. "My grandmother owned the house. My parents and brother and sister and I lived on the second floor. All the private houses on our street had originally been built by Henry Morgenthau, who was Secretary of the Treasury in Franklin Roosevelt's administration."

Hank's family moved to Coster Street in 1923, when he was a baby. At the time of his birth, the family had lived in another section of the Bronx. His parents, Samuel and Rose Ungerleider, were native New Yorkers—born on the Lower East Side of Manhattan. (Hank changed his name from Ungerleider to Leids.) His father worked in the Southern Boulevard station of the U.S. Post Office, which served Hunts Point.

"Back when I was a kid, there was an organization called the Hunts Point Civic Association that looked out for the neighborhood's interests," Hank recalls. "My father was an official of the civic association for a long time. The association was forever fighting to get traffic lights installed on Hunts Point Avenue—one at the intersection of Lafayette Avenue and the other at Bruckner Boulevard. They finally got the lights. I was by there not long ago, and I noticed that the lights are still there now."

The Hunts Point Civic Association, however, no longer exists. Like many of the organizations that helped provide Hunts Point with a community identity, it gradually crumbled and died. Its absence is all the more obvious today, when Hunts Point needs such an association more than ever in its history.

Hank's recollections of growing up in Hunts Point parallel in many ways those of Sherry. He recalls the same feelings of warmth and good-neighborliness she describes, and says he likewise has never lived anywhere else where he has run across comparable attitudes. "It was just a great place to grow up—a great place to live," he says.

Like Sherry, Hank attended Public School 48. Unlike her, however, he went there through the eighth grade. Boys attended the school from kindergarten through eighth grade, while girls left after the sixth grade to enter junior high. P.S. 48, besides having the numerical designation, was also called the Joseph Rodman Drake School—named for a prominent poet and satirist who lived in Hunts Point in the early 1800's. Drake, who was born in 1795 and died in 1820, is buried in a small cemetery set on a knoll at Hunts Point and Oak Point Avenues. Among his most famous poems was a tribute to the American flag that began:

When freedom from her mountain height
Unfurled her standard to the air,
She tore the azure robe of night
And set the stars of glory there.

He also wrote frequently about the glories of Hunts Point and other sections of the Bronx, including a poem that contained these lines:

Yet I will look upon thy face again,
My own romantic Bronx,
And it will be
A face more pleasant than the face of men.

One can only cringe at the ugliness Drake would find replacing that "pleasant face" if he visited Hunts Point today.

Not long ago, such ugliness invaded even the cemetery where Drake is buried. Young vandals swept through the cemetery at night, smashing tombstones and desecrating graves. In one of the few examples of community cooperation witnessed in Hunts Points in recent years, policemen stationed in the area and members of the Bronx County Historical Society organized a program to repair the damage. When it was finished, the cemetery was rededicated at ceremonies attended by more than a thousand children from P.S. 48. Some of the students planted a pin oak tree near the graves.

In the years when Sherry and Hank Leids lived in Hunts Point, an act such as the cemetery vandalism would have been unthinkable. Children involved in even minor accidents inflicting property damage were severely punished. "I remember, one time, I was playing touch football on the street outside P.S. 48," says Hank Leids. "Somebody made a bad pass and smashed one of the school windows. The principal, George Loughran, somehow found out I was involved. A few days later I was called down to Mr. Loughran's office. My father was waiting there; Mr. Loughran had called him. Mr. Loughran told my father what had happened, and before I could say a word, my father started beating the hell out of me right there in the office. Mr. Loughran just stood there and watched. I got down on the floor, trying to cover myself up with my arms, but my father didn't let up for about five minutes. I tell you, he really whipped the crap out of me. I never threw a football anywhere near that school again."

He did, however, play football and other sports elsewhere in Hunts Point. "We had a sandlot football team and we used to line up opposing teams by advertising in the *Bronx Home News*," Hank recalls. (The *Home News* was a daily newspaper that was eventually absorbed by the *New York Post*.) "We'd put an ad in the paper, saying how old our team was and how much our guys weighed, and we'd list a telephone number that other teams could call if they wanted to play us. The paper published the ads free. We'd get calls from all over the Bronx."

Hank played other sports in the streets or at the playground supervised by Berk Berkowitz. "I played on a paddle-tennis team that represented our playground in a citywide tournament sponsored by the Parks Department," he says. "We won the Bronx championship. Later, another team representing our playground won the city championship. I also played on a roller-skate hockey team—the Mercuries. I remember we had blue jerseys, with a yellow winged foot on the front. Mostly we just played in the streets. We made portable goals out of some netting. We'd have to move them out of the way every time a car came by. Once in a while we played in a Parks Department tournament against other teams from around the city."

After his graduation from P.S. 48, Hank attended James Monroe High School. With the outbreak of World War II, he entered the Army Signal Corps and saw combat duty in both the European and Pacific campaigns. He resumed his education after the war, attending New York University. By the time he met Sherry in 1951, the mass influx of Negroes and Latin-Americans had begun at Hunts Point, and his parents were among the many long-time residents preparing to flee from what they considered the horrors of a "changing neighborhood."

This was a critical period in Hunts Point's transition into a ghetto—a period when unscrupulous real-estate speculators, known as "blockbusters," were extremely active. Blockbusters are leeches who prey on the fears of white home-owners in changing neighborhoods. A typical blockbuster's technique is to approach a white home-owner and tell him something like this: "The niggers and spics are moving into the neighborhood. Soon it won't be safe here for you and your kids. They'll be all around you. Your property won't be worth anything. It's already dropped in value. But, if you want to get rid of it, I'll take it off your hands now—before it's too late. I'll give you a good price. Of course, it won't be what you could have gotten a few years ago—before these people started moving in. But it'll be a lot more than you'll get if you wait."

In many cases, residents whose families had lived in Hunts Point for generations succumbed to such panic-oriented appeals and sold out to the blockbusters. Most of them got only rock-bottom prices. The blockbusters then turned around and sold the homes at inflated prices to Negro and Latin-American families, or maintained ownership and converted the buildings into crowded apartment units.

Hank Leids and his parents moved from Hunts Point in 1952 to an apartment on the Grand Concourse, long one of the most fashionable streets in the Bronx. The following year, Hank and Sherry were married and moved in with Hank's parents. They later took their own apartment in the West Bronx, across town from Hunts Point, before moving to Long Island. Sherry's parents, however, remained in their small Hunts Point apartment.

"The neighborhood kept getting worse and worse," Sherry recalls. "I pleaded with my parents to leave, but they just wouldn't do it. They'd lived there so long that, as bad as it was, they preferred it to moving into a new environment. There were robberies all the time and drugs were all over the place. It got so they finally were living almost constantly behind locked doors—afraid to set foot outside. But they still refused to move. In 1965, my father was very ill and was taken to a hospital. We didn't know it at the time, but he was dying. I told him that, when he got out of the hospital, Hank and I wanted him and my mother to come and live with us on Long Island. Well, he died without ever coming home from the hospital. But after that, we finally persuaded my mother to leave Hunts Point. She came and lived with us for two years."

Later, her mother lived in Maryland with Sherry's brother,

Joe, before moving to Florida in 1971. It was because of an old Hunts Point friendship that Joe wound up in Maryland. "When we were kids, Joe had a friend in Hunts Point named Abe Shuster," Sherry says. "Abe's father owned a dry-cleaning store on Seneca Avenue, near the firehouse. When he grew up, Abe moved to Maryland and became very successful in the auto accessories business. He started a chain of shops called High Gear, which spread all over the state. He asked Joe to come down and run one of the shops. It worked out so well that Joe eventually became Abe's buyer."

Such stories involving Hunts Pointers are not uncommon. The close ties formed there, Sherry and Hank found, tended to transcend all other friendships they developed throughout their lives. Over the years, they have maintained their bonds with their Hunts Point contemporaries—even though, in some cases, they are now separated by hundreds of miles.

Sherry, in a nostalgic mood, casually ticks off the current whereabouts of many of her former neighbors. "Paul Prusky, who used to live in Apartment 3-C in our apartment house, is a surgeon up in Boston," she says. "Dotty Geller, who lived in Apartment 2-C, is a writer. She lives in New Rochelle. Shirley Finkelstein is a housewife in Queens. Janet Gold is a housewife in Westchester. Karen Becker married a Hunts Point boy whose family owned a big grocery business. She lives nearby on Long Island, in Northport. Myron Berman, who lived on Irvine Street, is a lawyer and lives in New Jersey. Arnie Klugerman, who lived on Seneca Avenue, is a businessman; he's married to a math teacher. They live in Manhattan. Sidney Shane lives in Maine and his brother, Marty, lives in Miami. We saw them not long ago down in Miami. Their sister, Helen, married a boy from Hunts Point named Bernie Weiss. Bernie is the brother of an actor who uses the stage name Simon Oakland. I saw him in a movie not long ago— *The Sand Pebbles*. Bernie and Simon's father used to own a candy store on Hunts Point Avenue.

"You know, quite a few people in show business come from Hunts Point. Tony Curtis, whose real name is Bernie Schwartz, lived around Simpson Street. Jan Murray, the comedian, lived nearby. And Milton Berle lived somewhere in the neighborhood, I'm not sure exactly where." (Another show-business personality from Hunts Point, whom Sherry neglected to mention, is tempestuous character actor Lionel Stander. An alumnus of P.S. 48, Stander was once the highest-paid supporting actor under contract to Columbia Pictures. After being blacklisted during Hollywood's Communist-hunting upheaval, he spent years in exile in Europe—but recently returned to the United States to play a Mafia boss in the film *The Gang That Couldn't Shoot Straight.*)

Not all of Sherry and Hank's old friends have left Hunts Point. One who has remained is Max Lasskow, who still lives in the private house at 650 Faile Street that his family has owned for decades. "When everybody else was moving out of Hunts Point, Max bought up a bunch of the houses in the neighborhood," Hank says. "He's made a lot of money—renting the houses to Negroes and Puerto Ricans. The property has kept him there. He's single, so he doesn't have to worry about having children grow up there."

Sherry and Hank return to Hunts Point occasionally to see Max Lasskow. "I don't know how he stands living there," Sherry says. "It's so depressing for me even to visit there that I can't wait to leave. The filth, the drugs, the fear—God, when I think of how beautiful Hunts Point used to be, it's heartbreaking!"

4

Al Rosenberg is twelve years younger than Hank Leids. For that reason, although they grew up in buildings only two blocks apart, Al's boyhood recollections of Hunts Point are considerably different from Hank's. During Al's youth, the neighborhood was undergoing its transition from the tranquil garden spot of Hank's childhood to the grim ghetto of today.

"It was beginning to become a tougher neighborhood," Al recalls. "Nothing like it is now, of course. But it was changing; no doubt about that. Puerto Ricans began moving in—a few at a time, then more and more. For the first time, street gangs began organizing. Crime and vandalism started to be problems. It happened gradually—not all at once."

Al, who now lives and teaches junior high school in Commack, Long Island, was born at Hunts Point Hospital. For the first six years of his life, however, he did not live in Hunts Point but in a nearby section of the Bronx. He and his parents, Samuel and Faye Rosenberg, then moved into an apartment house near Hunts Point Hospital—at 1275 Lafayette Avenue. His maternal grandparents, Samuel and Ray Cooper, lived nearby at 1290 Lafayette Avenue. After about five years, Al's family moved into Apartment 1-C at 754 Coster Street—a large triangular apartment house near the triple junction of Coster and Hunts Point and Lafayette Avenues.

The apartment was small, only three rooms, but it was all the family could afford on Samuel Rosenberg's salary as a textile salesman. In an adjacent apartment lived the twin basketball stars, Dick and Bill Kor. Although considerably older than Al Rosenberg, they befriended him and allowed him to tag along with them when he was a boy.

While the neighborhood was changing, remnants of the old Hunts Point were still intact. "There were still some farms and goat herds in the neighborhood as late as the early 1950's," Al says. "I remember that my father and I used to go fishing down at The Creek. Once, when we were walking home from there, we stopped to talk to the owner of a little farm near the cemetery where Joseph Rodman Drake is buried. He was a little old man with a heavy Italian accent. He'd been farming there for years—had a few goats and grew fruits and vegetables. He said he'd just brewed some homemade wine, and invited my father and me into his house to have some. It was powerful stuff."

Al attended P.S. 48 from kindergarten through the eighth grade. In keeping with Hunts Point's long-time "small town" character, the school had a degree of faculty stability that was highly unusual in New York City. Many of the teachers spent virtually their entire adult lives on the faculty, rejecting offers to transfer to other schools even when the neighborhood began undergoing radical change. Some taught several generations of the same family. A grammar teacher named Pauline Gernhardt, for example, taught at the school for more than a quarter of a century. Through her classroom passed children and occasionally even grandchildren of students she had taught during the World War I era. Similar experiences were encountered by such other long-time P.S. 48 teachers as Kathleen Brennan, Katherine Gleason, and Rose Dillon. A particular favorite of the male students was a math teacher named Abe Baras, who had a no-nonsense attitude but showed deep interest in Hunts Point boys even long after they had left the school.

"Mr. Baras just retired a few years ago," Al Rosenberg recalls. "He's living in Florida now. After he retired, I went to a testimonial dinner for him arranged by the Kor twins. I was amazed how many people from Hunts Point showed up. But he deserved it. He was a great teacher—a great guy."

It was during Al's years at P.S. 48 that the school, for the first time, became plagued with periodic acts of vandalism. "Once the tougher element began moving into the neighborhood, kids started breaking into the school at night," Al says. "Sometimes they'd steal something. But mostly they just tore the place apart."

Simultaneously, the entire neighborhood began to experience for the first time a general outbreak of burglaries, holdups, and other crimes. Compared with today's lawlessness in Hunts Point, that outbreak was relatively mild. But for a neighborhood where adherence to the law had always been traditional—one where it often seemed that the major police activity involved answering complaints about noisy stickball games—this new turn of events had all the impact of a major crime wave.

Meanwhile, another ominous sign developed with the emergence of teen-age street gangs. Such gangs, while common in other sections of the city, had never before sprung up in Hunts Point. A gang would carve out a turf for itself, usually an area of a few blocks in which its members lived, and defy teen-aged nonmembers to enter. Any who dared try were in danger of severe beatings or worse. Although zip guns were not yet fashionable among Hunts Point gangs in those days, switchblade knives, brass knuckles, and other potentially lethal weapons were prevalent. Occasionally, two gangs would tangle in a rumble, and the bloody victims would be hauled to hospitals afterward.

Al Rosenberg recalls that the most feared gang in the area was called the Jokers. It considered all of Hunts Point its turf, and its members delighted in roaming the streets—terrorizing teen-agers and adults alike. The Jokers operated an old-fashioned protection racket, accosting victims and forcing them to hand over all the money in their pockets or get beaten up. If a young victim was broke or had only a small amount of money on him, he was ordered to appear at an appointed time and place to pay up. Those who reneged found the Jokers hunting the neighborhood for them.

"I never had any personal problem with the Jokers because they knew I was friendly with the Kor twins," Al says. "They didn't want to tangle with the Kors, so they left me alone. But they beat the hell out of some other friends of mine."

Partly as a result of such beatings, and despite the fact that he had not been molested, Al joined with a handful of his friends in an informal group designed for mutual protection. It wasn't a street gang, Al emphasizes. It had no turf and made no aggressive forays against outsiders. "It was just a bunch of guys who hung out together and found safety in numbers," he says.

Not coincidentally, all members of the group were Jewish. They belonged to a youth organization that met at Temple Beth Elohim, a synagogue at the corner of Faile Street and Lafayette Avenue. Since most members of Hunts Point street gangs were Gentiles, the Jewish boys felt a special need to band together. This tendency was symptomatic of a larger trend then occurring in Hunts Point—the breakdown of the long-time melting-pot concept and consequent division of the population along ethnic and religious lines. The change did not occur suddenly. But gradually, as tensions and hostilities became more prevalent in the neighborhood, residents increasingly withdrew into groups composed of their own particular backgrounds. "Stay with your own kind," parents began instructing their children.

In school, Al Rosenberg and his Jewish friends were still thrown together with students of various backgrounds. But outside school they tended to isolate themselves from the others. When Al joined a neighborhood basketball team, for example, it was an all-Jewish team made up of members of the youth group that met at the synagogue. When he hung around on street corners, his companions were members of the same clique.

"We used to hang out at two candy stores," Al recalls. "One of them was Zack's, at Lafayette Avenue and Faile Street. The other was Saperstein's, on Bryant Avenue, just off Seneca Avenue. We'd just hang around there and crap around." (A "candy store," in New York parlance, is a shop that dispenses far more than candy. It usually serves as a combination luncheonette-newsstand-stationery store. In many cases, it is also the neighborhood's gathering place for youths who, in a more rural setting, might be known as drugstore cowboys.)

When he and his friends reached their mid-teens, Al says, they started spending much of their time as participants in a floating dice game that took place in the basements of various apartment houses on Faile Street and Bryant Avenue. "One night, for some reason, I wasn't there," he says. "It was lucky for me. The cops came charging in and broke up the game. They dragged all the guys down to night court. Some of us who hadn't been in the game heard about the raid and decided to go down to the court and see what happened. We must have gotten together five or six carloads of guys. When we got down to the courtroom, we all took seats in the spectators' section. Our friends were in the front of the courtroom, with the other prisoners. When the judge called their case, he told them: 'Stand up and face the court.' He meant to face him, but they thought he meant to face the people sitting in the courtroom. So they turned around, saw us sitting there, and started waving to us. The judge almost had a hemorrhage! But when he realized they'd never been in a court-room before and were just mixed-up—not real troublemakers—he fined them a few bucks each and let them go."

The existence of the floating crap game, while seemingly inconsequential, was also indicative of the change occurring in Hunts Point. In previous years, the highly disciplined teenagers in the neighborhood rarely did anything that put them in conflict with the law. While some of them may have committed minor offenses from time to time, they steered clear of anything as flagrant as a steady dice game. By Al Rosenberg's time, however, the discipline in the community was breaking down.

After the raid on the dice game, Al and his friends went looking for a spot more private than an apartment-house basement as a gathering place. "One of the guys, Jerry Schwartz, lived in a private house on Manida Street," Al says. "His family told us we could use the cellar of the house as a clubroom if we'd fix it up. So we cleaned the place up, painted it and decorated it, and formed a 'cellar club.' It was just a place to hang out and fool around. We'd take girls there, dance—that kind of thing."

When he was about sixteen, Al began dating a Hunts Point girl named Renee Salamon. Renee, who had moved to Hunts Point at the age of seven, lived in an apartment house at 868 Faile Street. After attending P.S. 48 and Junior High School 60, she had entered Morris High School. Al went to Stuyvesant High School, one of several New York City high schools that enrolled only unusually bright students. Since Stuyvesant was in Lower Manhattan, Al was required to make an hour-long subway ride each way. Despite the time-consuming travel and the long hours of study necessary to maintain his grades at Stuyvesant, he found time to continue his courtship of Renee.

During the early 1950's, as the character of Hunts Point continued to deteriorate, Al's parents grew increasingly disenchanted with the neighborhood. "More and more Puerto Ricans were moving in all the time," Al says. "There weren't too many Negroes in the neighborhood then, but there were Puerto Ricans all over the place—on Coster Street, Irvine Street, Garrison Avenue, and a bunch of other streets." Ultimately, the Rosenbergs decided to move out. "My father was making more money than he had in the past, so we could afford a little better apartment," Al recalls. The family took a four-room apartment on Ogden Avenue in the Highbridge section of the West Bronx, across town from Hunts Point.

Al continued dating Renee Salamon, and when he was twenty, they were married. Al got his bachelor's degree from New York University and his master's at City College of New York, then began work on a doctorate at St. John's University. Renee, after finishing one year of college, dropped out to become a full-time housewife. Al started teaching in New York City and was assigned to a succession of elementary schools in the Bronx. Several of them were in poverty-stricken Negro neighborhoods, but conditions there were still several notches above those that had developed in Hunts Point.

Nonetheless, he found teaching in such schools so depressing that he decided to seek a job outside the city school system. He landed one in the Northport, Long Island, school district and bought a house in nearby Commack. After five years in Northport, he was offered a principal's job in Westwood, New Jersey. Unable to find a house in his price range in the Westwood area, he drove two hours each way between Commack and the New Jersey school for a year. Then, finding the commuting too much of a grind, he gave up the job as principal and became a developmental reading teacher at Green Meadows Junior High in Commack.

Like Sherry and Hank Leids, Al Rosenberg has maintained some contact over the years with people still in Hunts Point and friends from the neighborhood who have long since moved elsewhere. "One of my uncles is a doctor who still has his office in Hunts Point," Al says. "His name is Dr. Herman Seidman; he's had his office for years at 760 Hunts Point Avenue. He used to live in Hunts Point, but now he has a big house in Scarsdale. He made enough money treating welfare patients in Hunts Point to be able to afford to live in Scarsdale."

Many of Al's old Hunts Point friends, like those of Sherry and Hank Leids, are now spread far and wide—some as distant as Israel and the Soviet Union. "One of the guys, Tony Astrachan, is the Moscow correspondent for the *Washington Post*," Al says. "Tony's brother, Sam, is also a writer. He's had several books published. One of them, I remember, was called *An End to Dying*. Another guy, Harris Schenker, went to live in Israel. Dick and Bill Kor both live in New Rochelle; they're physical education teachers. Another friend of mine, Larry Stoner, who used to live on Faile Street, is in the home-building business in Sarasota, Florida. His mother, May Stoner, was assistant principal for many years at Junior High School 60. Until a short time ago, a fellow from Hunts Point named Marty Lebow lived right near here in Commack. He's an automobile salesman. He moved somewhere else on Long Island."

Not infrequently, Al says, he accidentally runs across a former Hunts Pointer and renews an interrupted friendship. "A short time ago I was visiting somebody in Bayside [a section of the borough of Queens]," he says. "Who should I run into but a guy from Hunts Point named Stanley Chimkin? He's a big, husky guy—used to be one of the tough guys at P.S. 48. What do you think he's doing now? He's a hairdresser! I couldn't believe it. He looks like a professional wrestler, but he's a hairdresser."

When the Rosenbergs left Hunts Point—along with the Astrachans, the Schenkers, the Kors, the Stoners, the Lebows, the Chimkins, and countless others—who replaced them? Who are the Hunts Pointers of today? Why did they come there? How do they live? And what lies ahead for them? These questions, and others, will be confronted in succeeding chapters.

Jesus Seijo stares warily through the peep-
hole in the front door of his fourth-floor
apartment at 875 Longfellow Avenue—
where Sherry Leids lived with her parents

5

two decades ago. Assured that the person who has
rung his doorbell poses no threat, Jesus opens three
door locks and ushers the visitor inside. "This is a
very rough neighborhood," he says apologetically.
"People are getting robbed and killed all the time. I don't
open my door unless I'm sure it's OK."

A short, slender man of fifty, Jesus appears frail and vul-
nerable as he stands there with his feet and chest bare, wearing only a pair of paint-spattered khaki slacks. In his hand is
an unlighted cigarette, the last of a pack, which he will hold
for more than a half-hour before finally allowing himself the
luxury of lighting up. "Let me show you something," he says.
He leads the way to a large metal box hanging on a hallway
wall, then pushes a button on the side of the box. *Bong!*
Bong! Bong! Bong! Bong! Bong! Bong! An alarm bell, loud
enough to be heard a half-block away, rings incessantly until
Jesus cuts it off.

"I keep that there to scare robbers away," he says. "That's
the kind of thing you have to do to protect yourself in this
neighborhood." Leading from the alarm box is a wire that

connects with another push-button device near the inside of the front door. "I can set the alarm off from two different places," Jesus explains. "If there's any kind of trouble, I'll run to the closest button and start that bell ringing like hell."

While such measures afford partial protection from Hunts Point's marauding thieves when Jesus, his wife, and two children are in their apartment, the danger escalates once they set foot outside. "I've been hit in the head and robbed twice in the last couple of months—right in the lobby of this building," Jesus says. "I work nights, and I was on my way to work both times. It's not safe to carry much money around here at night, so I just had a few dollars in my pocket. One time, five guys jumped me. One of them hit me on the head with a piece of pipe or something. I fell down and they took the money out of my pocket and ran. The other time, it was just a couple of guys—but they did the same thing. I was lucky they didn't kill me."

Almost daily, Jesus says, there are reminders of the violence that lurks everywhere in Hunts Point. "The other day, I went into a store that cashes paychecks for people in the neighborhood. Another man came in and cashed a big check. As he walked out the door, a guy standing on a roof across the street fired a carbine at him. Luckily the shot missed. The guy with the carbine ran away. He had two other guys working with him. They were on the street, and they ran away with him. They must have known the man who came into the store was gonna cash a big check. I guess if the shot hit him, the two guys on the street would have grabbed his money."

Why, in view of all the hazards, do Jesus and his family live in Hunts Point? "It's all we can afford," he replies. "The rent is $80.49 a month. If I could pay more, we'd move somewhere else tomorrow—but I can't."

Jesus was born and reared in a rural area in northern Puerto Rico. He emigrated to New York in 1946. He has lived at 875 Longfellow Avenue with his wife, Herminia, twenty-seven, and their eight-year-old son, David, and six-year-old daughter, Ibelisse, for the last five years. Before that, the family lived for three years in another Hunts Point building at 726 Coster Street.

"This building is not very good, but it's better than the one on Coster Street," Jesus says. Outside the apartment house, can upon can of foul-smelling garbage lines the sidewalk. It has been there for days, and there is no telling when it will be picked up by city sanitation workers. A fire hydrant opened by neighborhood children three days earlier has still not been closed. It sends torrents of water cascading through the street, overflowing the sewers and creating a swamp of muck in the gutter.

Inside his apartment, however, Jesus tries to see the sunny side of his family's situation. He points proudly to the freshly painted walls of a small room where David and Ibelisse sit before a flickering television screen. "I couldn't get the landlord to paint the room, so I painted it myself," he says. "We try to keep the apartment nice. It's not fancy, but we keep it clean. It's not so bad." On the ceiling above the children there is a wet spot about three feet square. "Water leaks from the plumbing upstairs," Jesus explains. "We can't get the landlord to fix it." Then he shrugs and repeats: "It's not so bad."

When David and Ibelisse are not in school, they spend most of their time in the apartment. For hour after hour, they sit in front of the television set. The kinds of attitudes Sherry Leids recalls from her years in the apartment house—with residents frequently visiting each other's apartments and children forming lifelong friendships—are absent today. "We don't know anybody in the building," Jesus says. "People don't go out of their apartments unless they have to; they're too scared. How can you make friends when things are like that?" Because of the danger in the streets, David and Ibelisse are not permitted to wander the neighborhood or stroll

[43]

along the Bronx River the way Sherry used to do. They, their parents, and countless other present-day Hunts Pointers are, in effect, self-imprisoned in their homes much of the time—venturing outside only when necessary.

Jesus feels he risks his life every time he leaves the apartment at night to go to his job as a manufacturing worker at a Ronzoni Macaroni factory. "If somebody comes after me at night, there's nobody else around to help me," he says. "There are no cops on the streets. There are no cab drivers; they won't come into this area. I'm just on my own, and it scares the hell out of me."

Except for working the night shift, Jesus likes his job. The wages aren't high, he says, but they're enough to enable the family to "get by." He gently pats his wife's stomach, pointing out that she is pregnant. "When the baby comes, things will be a little harder," he says. "But we'll manage."

In the two-family red brick house where Hank Leids used to live, at 634 Coster Street, there now resides a family headed by seventy-three-year-old Alister Cox. A short, jolly man with skin the color of light cocoa, Cox is a native of the island of St. Lucia in the West Indies. He came to the United States in 1921 and lived in Harlem until 1952, when he bought the Coster Street house from Hank Leids' family.

Wearing slacks, a T-shirt, and bedroom slippers, Cox sits on a worn daybed on the second floor of the house and reminisces—his soft voice filled with the singsong lilt of the Indies. Before his retirement in 1961, he worked for eighteen years as a merchant seaman. "I shipped mostly on freighters," he says. "I loved the sea. I went all over the world—Germany, Russia, England, Spain, Cuba, Africa."

Now, like the family of Jesus Seijo and many other Hunts Pointers, he is forced by hazardous surroundings to spend much of his time inside his home. He takes consolation, however, from the fact that he is surrounded by many of his loved ones. "This is a family house," Cox says. He and his wife, Clara, share the house with one unmarried child, three married children, their spouses, and four grandchildren. They have another married child and three other grandchildren who live elsewhere.

"This neighborhood sure has changed since we moved here," Cox says, shaking his head. "When we came, most of our neighbors were Italians or Jews. Now, they're mostly Puerto Ricans. Of course, it's a much rougher neighborhood now. When we came here, we didn't even have to lock our doors; we just left them wide open. But we can't do that any more. We keep them locked tight, day and night. It used to be that people kept trees and gardens and looked after their property—but now they just let everything go to pot."

Like Jesus Seijo, Cox says he hardly knows any of his neighbors. "When we first moved here, I was away at sea a lot of the time, so I didn't get friendly with anybody," he explains. By the time of his retirement, the area had deteriorated so badly that he was reluctant to leave his home any more than necessary, even to get acquainted with his close neighbors.

The Cox home has never been victimized by thieves—apparently because there are so many members of the family living there that someone is home all the time. "We've been lucky," Cox says. "We get lots of phone calls where the person on the other end hangs up as soon as we answer. I'm sure many of them are from thieves, checking to see if we're home." His neighbors, however, have not been so lucky. Many of their homes have been burglarized, some as often as four or five times.

Cox blames the city government for deepening the deterioration of Hunts Point. "The city doesn't take care of this neighborhood," he says. "Days and days go by without the garbage being picked up. And you almost never see a policeman around here. Every two weeks or so, you might see one passing through. This neighborhood needs far more attention from the city than the average neighborhood. Instead, it gets far less. In fact, it gets hardly any at all."

A block and a half from the Cox home is the city playground where "Berk" Berkowitz used to be recreation supervisor. A visit to the playground discloses the type of governmental neglect described by Cox. It is a hot summer day, and local children are off from school. Yet, at midday, there is no city employee on duty at the playground. Not one child is playing there. A handful of adults, several of whom appear to be high on narcotics, lounge on park benches. For years, neighborhood residents had pleaded with city officials to build a large swimming pool in Hunts Point. After long turning them down, the city finally threw them a crumb—installing a tiny pool in the playground. To make room for the pool, the city eliminated the basketball court where the Kor twins and countless other Hunts Point athletes had learned the sport. On the day the playground was visited, the pool—which is surrounded by a tall chain-link fence—was locked. Why? There was nobody on duty to say. Like so much else in Hunts Point, it was going to waste.

Nearby, at 754 Coster Street, is the five-story walkup apartment house where Al Rosenberg used to live. In an apartment on the ground floor, formerly occupied by Al and his parents, Felix Rivera now lives with his wife, Matilda. Felix, who is fifty-seven, serves as the building's superintendent. A native of Ponce, Puerto Rico, he moved to New York in 1951 and has lived in the Hunts Point area for ten years. He has been the superintendent of the Coster Street building for seven years. Before that he lived for three years on Hoe Avenue, a street on the opposite end of Hunts Point from Coster. Although all of Hunts Point is ravaged and dangerous, some streets are considered worse than others. Hoe Avenue is considered among the worst of all. "Coster is bad, but Hoe is really a jungle," Felix says. "There's no security there at all. The junkies have completely taken it over."

While his move to Coster Street was a slight step upward, Felix says there is no telling how long it will remain any better than Hoe Avenue. "It's getting worse all the time," he says. "There are a lot of crazy people around here. They have no respect for anything. It seems like there are more criminals and more narcotics around here every day."

As protection against thieves, he keeps his apartment door secured with a device consisting of a heavy length of pipe that is wedged between the lock and a metal anchor on the floor. It is virtually impossible to open the door unless the pipe is removed. Felix is also responsible for trying to provide a measure of security to the tenants, but has had only moderate success. "When I find someone hanging around the lobby or the hallways who doesn't belong in the building, I try to chase him," he says. "But I've got other work to do; I can't keep everyone out. Just last week, two black guys came in and grabbed an old man in one of the hallways and beat him up and robbed him."

Felix tells the familiar story of fear in Hunts Point—that tenants in his building remain in their apartments as much as possible. "They just stay to themselves," he says. "They don't visit back and forth. They don't even know each other most of the time. They're scared even when they're inside their apartments, but they're scared worse when they have to go out."

In their own apartment, Felix and his wife appear relatively comfortable. The place is clean, the furniture polished. In the living room, the armchairs and sofa are covered with protective plastic. Elsewhere in the building, however, some apartments are filthy and cluttered. The furniture is ancient and ramshackle. Many of the tenants seem devoid of pride or hope. "I don't know what can be done for these people," Felix says. "I just don't know."

About a block away, in a building across the street from P.S. 48, people *are* trying to do something to improve the lot of the residents of Hunts Point. The building houses the Hunts Point Spanish Presbyterian Church. It also doubles as the headquarters of the Hunts Point Head Start Program. Operation Head Start is a federally funded program that offers preschool educational preparation to ghetto children, and health and social services to them and their families.

Mrs. Martha Watford, administration director of the Hunts Point headquarters, complains that shortages of money, facilities, and space force her staff to provide only a fraction of the services the community needs. "Every year, we have to fight for money," she says. "And every year, we don't get enough." The current annual budget for the Hunts Point program is $103,000. "We get more than two hundred applications a year for four-year-old children to take part in the pre-kindergarten program," Mrs. Watford says. "Under our budget, we're supposed to take just sixty children. Actually, we're managing to squeeze in sixty-eight. But even so, we're turning down more children than we accept."

Those children accepted are given instruction to prepare them for such subjects as reading, arithmetic, science, and social studies when they enter grade school. They are also taken on field trips to points of interest in the city. One underlying theory of the Head Start program is that ghetto children, because of the deprived educational and cultural backgrounds of their families, often are ill-prepared to begin school when they reach kindergarten age. The hope is that Head Start will help bring them up to levels where they can proceed in school at a comparable pace with children from more advantaged backgrounds. But the instruction of the children is only part of the overall program, says Mrs. Emma Louro, a family assistant at the Hunts Point headquarters. "We try to involve the whole family," she explains. "We try to motivate these families—many of them welfare families—to do things for themselves."

The program staff includes, in addition to three certified

teachers, such other specialists as a psychologist, family counselors, and social workers. The staff can also obtain help from various governmental agencies, such as the City Board of Health. "Hunts Point lacks many facilities, and one of the things it lacks most is medical service," Mrs. Louro says. "We arrange for the Board of Health to provide us with doctors to give complete medical examinations to all the children involved in our program. For some of them, these are the only medical examinations they ever get. The doctors make tests for such things as sickle-cell anemia, measles, and lead poisoning." (Sickle-cell anemia is a hereditary disease, generally confined to Negroes, that causes clogging of blood vessels. Lead poisoning is a condition prevalent among children in ghetto areas. It often results from the children eating chips of dried, lead-based paint from the walls of their homes.)

"We also provide other services," says Mrs. Louro. "We help people with their housing problems, their problems with welfare agencies—things like that. We have a number of committees that work on community problems—a nutrition committee, a cultural committee, a financial committee, a parents' council. We try to get as many people from the community involved as we can."

Besides Operation Head Start, other anti-poverty programs are functioning with varying degrees of success in Hunts Point. Some of them will be discussed later in this book. All suffer from similar problems—most notable among them what Mrs. Watford charges is a tendency by government officials to give Hunts Point far less than its share of aid.

"This is a forgotten area," she complains. "Why can't people in this area get the same services everybody else gets? Why can't they get their garbage collected? Why can't they get adequate police protection? Why can't they get decent housing? Why can't they get sufficient medical service? Why can't their kids go to decent schools? Why are Hunts Point kids automatically assigned tu vocational high schools, even when they're qualified to go to academic high schools? Hunts Point Hospital was torn down last year. We've been trying to get a community center put on that site, but nobody pays any attention to us. Why can't we get a community center there?"

Asked what it would take to rehabilitate Hunts Point, Mrs. Watford replies: "The main thing is for public officials to change their attitude about the people in Hunts Point. They assume we're all narcotics addicts, prostitutes, and criminals. They feel we're ignorant and don't know what living is all about. They've got to recognize us as human beings and not second-class citizens."

6

Mention the name Hunts Point to an outsider who knows something about the area and he invariably conjures up an image of crime, danger, and violence. To him, it is usually a vague, abstract image. But to the person living in Hunts Point, the crime, violence, and danger are quite specific. Every Hunts Pointer has his own horror story to tell. If he hasn't personally been victimized, then one of his close relatives or friends has been. Or perhaps he has been an eyewitness to an act of terror.

Thus, one cannot hope to appreciate the full impact of crime on Hunts Point by considering the problem only in mass, general terms. One must, instead, confront specific cases—keeping in mind that each victim and each criminal is a flesh-and-blood human being and not a mere statistic. What follows is a brief recounting of a series of crimes committed within a period of months. Most took place in Hunts Point. A few were committed by Hunts Pointers outside their home neighborhood, but were nonetheless significant because they indicated the influence of the area's criminal element on New York City as a whole. For every crime described here, it is important to note that there were hundreds of others involving Hunts Pointers during the same period. Those discussed reflect a representative sample.

It is 10:15 P.M. Joseph Daren, five years old, sits with his mother, Mrs. Mary Daren, thirty-four, on a living-room couch in their third-floor apartment at 1231 Stebbins Avenue. They are watching television. The Darens are the only occupants of the entire tenement, since all the other decrepit apartments have been abandoned. Crack! Crack! Suddenly, for no apparent reason, two bullets are fired through the wooden door of the Daren apartment. Both slam into the left side of Joseph's stomach. The senseless, inexplicable shooting leaves him critically wounded. His assailant flees from the tenement hallway and escapes.

Antonio Alemany, thirty-two, is arrested on a Hunts Point street on a charge of kidnaping a thirteen-year-old boy. The boy has escaped from Alemany's car, has run to the Police Department's 41st Precinct station house at 1086 Simpson Street to report the crime, and has led detectives back to the car. After his arrest, Alemany is taken to the station house for questioning. Officers discover he has a record of three previous arrests on charges of assault, burglary, and endangering the welfare of a child. Alemany is led into a squad room to be fingerprinted by Detective Joseph A. Picciano. Without warning, while his prints are being taken, Alemany grabs the detective and tries to seize his service revolver. In the struggle, the gun drops to the floor. Two other detectives in the room, Joseph Marrero and Richard Ware, shout to Picciano: "Get your gun!" But Alemany gets it instead, fires two quick shots into Picciano's chest, then sprays the squad room with bullets. Detectives Marrero and Ware, taking cover beneath tables, return the fire. Another detective, William Lally, hears the shots and rushes in from another room. He fires four shots into Alemany's throat and wrist. When the smoke clears, both Alemany and Detective Picciano are dead. The detective, a veteran of eleven years on the police force, leaves a widow and three children.

Not far from the station house, Patrolman Joseph Perez, now off-duty, walks along Simpson Street shortly after two A.M. He has just finished his shift and is on his way home. Before starting work he had cashed both his paycheck and a tax-refund check, so he has $1,300 in his pocket. As he passes 960 Simpson Street, three men jump from the shadows, grab him at knife-point, and force him into a hallway of the building. They take his money and his service revolver, then flee in different directions. Although Perez is in uniform and within shouting distance of the station house, the robbery is not considered particularly audacious by Hunts Point standards. As for Perez, he counts himself lucky that he emerged from the incident physically unharmed.

Albert Epstein, fifty-one-year-old landlord of an apartment house at 1132 Kelly Street, is disturbed because the New York rent-control law prevents him from raising his tenants' rents. If the current tenants move out, however, he can charge higher rents to those who take their places. When harassment of the tenants fails to persuade them to move, Epstein hits on a plan to force them out of the building. He'll get someone to set the five-story building on fire. He figures to make a two-way profit from the arson scheme: first, he'll collect fire insurance; second, he'll repair the building and rent the apartments to new tenants at increased rates. Epstein hires a former tenant, Benjamin Warren, to carry out the arson plot. Warren, in turn, recruits three teen-aged boys to help him set the fire. Once the fire is raging, to make certain that the boys will never inform on him, Warren locks them inside a burning room. All three die in the blaze. The police eventually uncover the plot and arrest both Warren and Epstein. Warren gets twenty years in prison for murder and arson; Epstein gets an indeterminate sentence up to ten years for arson.

A Hunts Point street gang known as the Savage Nomads goes on a two-day rampage—destroying property and terrorizing residents along Vyse Avenue. The disorder mounts constantly in intensity, and finally leads to the fatal stabbing of fifty-one-year-old Sylvester Latham of 1168 Vyse Avenue. An eighteen-year-old member of the Savage Nomads, Raphael Rosario of 1206 Westchester Avenue, is indicted on murder charges. But the Savage Nomads and other street gangs continue to wage campaigns of terror in Hunts Point. Only occasionally do older residents dare to retaliate against the young gang members. One such case occurs when a gang called the Savage Skulls runs wild near the intersection of Kelly Street and Intervale Avenue. Members of the gang previously have been stealing beer from a grocery store there. When the store owner tries to halt the thievery, the Savage Skulls decide to demonstrate their power both to him and to other residents of the neighborhood. About thirty gang members—armed with Molotov cocktails, clubs, and bricks—descend upon the intersection one night. They throw two Molotov cocktails through the glass door of the grocery. They then run down Kelly Street, hurling other fire bombs indiscriminately and chasing older people from sidewalks and stoops into their tenements. But one group of neighborhood residents—made up mostly of men in their thirties—decides to resist. Wading into the swarm of Savage Skulls, the men grab four of the biggest gang members and proceed to beat the daylights out of them. Other members of the gang flee. The men later retreat into their homes and prepare for an avenging raid by the Savage Skulls. Thus far the raid has not come, but Hunts Pointers are certain it will one day. Meanwhile, warfare erupts between the Savage Skulls on one side and two gangs called the Black Spades and the Seven Immortals on the other. There is a brawl in a movie theater. A student at John Dwyer Junior High School,

Hermino Medera, is severely beaten in the school yard in the aftermath of the theater brawl. Robert Benjamin (Black Benjy) Cornell, twenty-five-year-old leader of another gang, called the Ghetto Brothers, tries to mediate the dispute and bring an end to the violence. "Let's make peace, brothers," he tells members of the warring gangs who are gathered outside the school. Instead of making peace, various teen-agers set upon Cornell with iron pipes, knives, boards, and other weapons. He is beaten and stabbed to death. Police arrest one eighteen-year-old, George Peterson, on a homicide charge and press the hunt for Cornell's other purported assailants. Still, members of the rival gangs vow to continue the warfare.

Carlos Feliciano, forty-one, a militant Puerto Rican nationalist, is seized by police as he tries to plant a bomb in an army recruiting station at one of Hunts Point's main intersections—163rd Street and Southern Boulevard. The police, who have been following Feliciano, say he kept the bomb hidden inside a hollowed-out loaf of French bread. They search his car and find a second bomb. Later, they charge him with a total of thirty-five bombings, ranging from Hunts Point to the main building of the New York Public Library in Manhattan.

Orlando Rodriguez and his wife, Jenny, owe $1,300 to Benjamin Olivio. Despite Olivio's repeated attempts to collect, the debt drags on for about five years. Finally, Olivio decides to take the money at gun-point, if necessary. Backed by his twenty-year-old son, Benjamin, Jr., and two other youths—Anselmo Detres, twenty, and Richard Frejomil, nineteen—Olivio confronts the Rodriguezes and demands repayment. An argument ensues and escalates into gunplay. Mrs. Rodriguez is killed and her husband is wounded. The two Olivios, Detres, and Frejomil are indicted on charges of murder and attempted murder.

A one-year-old girl, Annette McCray of 1057 Simpson Street, dies under mysterious circumstances. An autopsy discloses that she has been beaten to death. Investigating detectives discover evidence that the beating has been administered by Annette's father, Anthony McCray. He is arrested on manslaughter charges.

A man is beaten and stabbed in a brawl. Two men suspected of taking part in the assault—Frank Vega, forty-one, and Antonio Garcia, twenty-three—are secretly followed back to Vega's apartment by about fifteen of the victim's friends. In the fourth-floor apartment at 967 Aldus Street, which police later describe as a heroin "shooting gallery," a party is in progress. Seven or eight persons are milling around. Suddenly the door bursts open and the fifteen friends of the beating victim rush in, brandishing shotguns, pistols, and knives. Three of them grab Vega's common-law wife, twenty-three-year-old Vickie Rivera, and drag her into a bathroom. There they take turns raping her. Meanwhile, other members of the raiding party force Vega and Garcia to undress and hand over their money. When the rapists return from the bathroom, they and their friends attack Vega and Garcia—beating both of them, stabbing Garcia in the chest and back, and shooting Vega in the chest. As they prepare to leave the apartment, Miss Rivera emerges from the bathroom. One of the invaders levels a shotgun at her and fires once. The blast strikes her in the heart and kills her. Vega and Garcia are rushed to a hospital in critical condition. The attackers escape.

The American Bank Note Company operates a plant at Hunts Point that prints, among other things, large amounts of foreign currency. One day, $209,600 worth of Mexican currency—in denominations ranging from 20-peso notes to 500-peso notes—is stolen from the plant. Internal accounting procedures disclose the loss within hours. Detectives receive information that a company employee, Arthur Green, Jr., twenty-six, is suspected of throwing a suspicious bundle out a plant window on the day of the theft. Green is shadowed for three weeks and ultimately leads the detectives to the office of Carlton Brown, fifty-one, publisher of a Harlem social magazine named *Cool*. The detectives raid the office, find the stolen currency, and arrest the two men.

Since many New York taxi drivers refuse to enter Hunts Point for fear of their lives, the area gets sporadic taxi service from a number of so-called "gypsy" cab companies operating without the normal city licensing and regulation. Radames Toro, a twenty-three-year-old "gypsy" cab driver, is hailed about one-thirty one morning by three teen-aged boys at the intersection of Southern Boulevard and Hoe Avenue. He picks them up and is told to drive to an address several miles away. But after he has gone only a few blocks, one of the passengers whips out a pistol and shouts: "This is a stickup!" When Toro fumbles in an attempt to produce his money, the passenger fires a shot into his back. The assailant and his companions leap from the moving cab, then flee on foot. Toro loses control of the cab, which crashes into a parked car. He is rushed to a hospital in critical condition. There, he manages to give police a description of his passengers. He says they may be as young as fifteen.

Antoinette Dishman, a seventeen-year-old Barnard College freshman, attends a party that starts in Manhattan and then moves to the Bronx. During the party she is given a dose of heroin by a Hunts Point man, Harold Burnel, twenty-seven. A short time later she collapses and dies. An autopsy discloses the cause of death as an overdose of the drug. Burnel, arrested on a charge of negligent homicide, pleads guilty and is sentenced to three years in prison.

Mrs. Margaret Hajos, a seventy-five-year-old widow, lives in a five-story tenement on Simpson Street. She scrapes by on monthly checks of $89.20 from Social Security and $44.90 from a union pension fund. Somehow, she saves $256 and buys an eighteen-inch television set to help her while away the long hours in her apartment. One day, she walks out on the front steps of the building for a few minutes. By the time she returns, thieves have broken into her apartment and made off with the TV set. But that is not the end of her troubles. A short time later water comes rushing into her apartment through the ceiling, seeps down the walls, and forms a lake several inches deep on the floor. "The junkies," Mrs. Hajos explains. "They stole the pipes from a vacant apartment upstairs. All the water came down here." The flooding stops only when all the water in the building is cut off. Mrs. Hojas is then left without any running water for several weeks, and finally moves to the building next door. Asked why she doesn't move clear out of Hunts Point, she replies: "No. My father always told me, 'You've gotta be tougher than they are.' I stay."

Two Hunts Point men—Carlos Rosado, thirty-five, who lives on Hoe Avenue, and George L. Colon, thirty, who lives on Seneca Avenue—draw the suspicion of detectives by loitering outside a bank. When an elderly man named Bill Rosen emerges from the bank with a package containing what appears to be a cash payroll, Rosado and Colon follow him. They, in turn, are tailed by Detectives Louis Gonzales, Henry Jacob, and Edwin Gilmurray. Rosen enters an office building and steps into a self-service elevator, then is quickly joined by Rosado and Colon. The detectives remain in the lobby. As the elevator rises to an upper floor, Rosado and Colon draw guns and force Rosen to give them his package. Actually, it does not contain a payroll—merely a batch of bank receipts for more than $3,000—but the robbers do not learn that immediately. When they descend in the elevator with the package, the detectives are waiting for them. "Freeze!" one of the detectives orders. But Colon and Rosado whip out their guns and open fire, touching off a blazing gun battle. By the time it ends, Detective Gonzales falls with a bullet wound in the left thigh, as does Rosado, and Colon is shot once in each thigh. All three are hospitalized, and Rosado and Colon are later jailed.

A ring of thieves makes a specialty of stealing welfare checks from the mailboxes of homes and apartment houses in Hunts Point. Within a period of months, more than $500,000 worth of checks are stolen. Two members of the ring, Milton Ramirez and Miguel A. Rodriguez, are arrested and plead guilty to federal conspiracy charges. Three businessmen accused of cashing the stolen checks at a discount are also arrested. At their trial, they claim they accepted the checks in the normal course of business without knowing they had been stolen. The businessmen are found not guilty.

Ebb Glenn, a twenty-three-year-old Negro who lives at 833 Longfellow Avenue and works in the account executives' department of an advertising agency, joins a militant black group accused of plotting "to kill a cop a week." The group is infiltrated by two black undercover policemen. They obtain evidence, including secretly made tape recordings disclosing that the group plans to raid a National Guard armory in the Bronx to obtain weapons for use in its plot to assassinate policemen. The undercover men also discover that

Glenn and other members of the group already possess a number of guns and bombs. Police arrest Glenn and four other members of the group, charging them with conspiracy and illegal possession of the guns and bombs. Four of the five defendants, including Glenn, are convicted. Glenn and one codefendant are sentenced to one to three years in prison; the other two convicted men are put on probation for five years.

Police receive information that a major car-theft ring is operating out of a Hunts Point auto-wrecking yard at 432 Faile Street. To maintain surveillance over the yard, detectives establish a secret lookout post in a small cubicle atop P.S. 48. They use telescopes, binoculars, and cameras with long-range lenses to gather evidence against the ring. With walkie-talkies, they direct the deployment of plainclothesmen on the streets below, who are assigned to note the license numbers of cars taken into the yard. The investigation discloses that the ring is responsible for the theft of at least a thousand cars. At the wrecking yard, the autos are dismantled and their parts are then sold to repair shops for prices ranging from $1,000 to $1,500 per car. One of the ring's chief customers is found to be a used-car dealer in Gerre, South Carolina. The investigation also discloses that at least five policemen are implicated in the ring's operations. Ultimately, a Bronx grand jury indicts seventeen men, including the five policemen and the owners of the wrecking yard, Michael J. Doris and Stephen Callinan. Three of the indicted policemen —Sergeant Thomas E. Quigley, Detective Jerome M. Dowling, and Patrolman Robert A. McAllister—are accused of taking $5,000 from a ring member in return for not arresting him. A fourth officer, Sergeant Philip J. Knecht, is charged with accepting a $2,300 bribe from two other ring members. The fifth policeman, Patrolman Joseph V. Savino, is accused of actually being a member of the ring and working in his off-duty hours as an auto-cutter at the wrecking yard. At this writing, McAllister was found not guilty and Quigley and Dowling were found guilty. Charges against all other defendants are still pending.

Two murders in Hunts Point in late 1971 spurred the formation of a citizens' committee aimed at spearheading a nationwide campaign against violent crime. On September 2, a forty-eight-year-old automobile dealer, Seymour Schneider, was shot to death in his office at 1489 Bruckner Boulevard by one or more robbers who stole a few hundred dollars from him. From all indications, Schneider had offered no resistance and had been murdered wantonly and senselessly. Several weeks later, in a crime equally senseless, a seventy-two-year-old dentist, Dr. Isidore Gelb, was robbed and shot to death in his Lafayette Avenue office. Violent death in Hunts Point is so commonplace that neither murder was covered by New York's major news media.

Schneider's brother, Peter, an attorney who had served as a policeman for ten years, was so saddened and angered by his family's tragedy that he wrote a biting but moving article about it for the opposite-editorial page of the *New York Times*.

I wish to report that my brother has been murdered. On the afternoon of September 2, 1971—a few days short of his forty-ninth birthday—my brother, Seymour Schneider, who in his lifetime had never raised a hand in violence against another, was shot in the head twice and robbed in his auto sales office on Bruckner Boulevard in the Bronx. The lives of many will be diminished because of his death—his wife to whom he was devoted, his children to whom he was dedicated, his brothers and sisters to whom he was loyal, his relatives and friends to whom he brought a lightness of spirit, a measure of joy, and a manner that was carefree, though his life was not. But from all the rest of the world he slipped silently away, in spite of the sound of the bullets that shattered his skull, for his murder was not deemed worthy of note in our press. A man is killed in broad daylight in his street-floor office on a main roadway in the city, and compounding the horror of the homicide is that, outside of his family and friends, the event is unnoticed. Murder has become commonplace. It has joined the crimes of mugging and rape in occurring with such frequency that newspapers seldom report them. When I went to the medical examiner's office to identify his body, I was given a number to await my turn as we are given numbers in a busy retail shop. Fifteen hundred such murders a year, many thousands of vicious muggings on our streets and in the lobbies of our houses, and with it all we go through the routine of daily existence. How long can people survive in this jungle of violence, terror, and fear? How many more casualties must we suffer before we recognize that we cannot live this way? Two of my three sisters have been mugged and assaulted, and now one of my brothers has been murdered and robbed. Who is next in this game of New York roulette?

The publication of Peter Schneider's article and his subsequent appearance on a radio talk show prompted more than five thousand persons to write him, expressing sentiments similar to his own. Through these letters, he learned of the murder of Dr. Gelb. By coincidence, more than thirty years earlier, Peter Schneider had dealt with Dr. Gelb's brother, Sol, an attorney and one-time judge of the New York Court of General Sessions. The two lawyers renewed acquaintances to discuss the murders of their brothers and what could be done to curb crime in Hunts Point, other sections of New York, and the nation at large. They were later joined in their discussions by a third man whose brother had been murdered, James W. Ballow, an administrator in the New York City Real Estate Department. Ballow's brother, George, a utility company foreman, had been slain by a sniper while working in Manhattan in 1970.

The conversations among the three men led to the formation in late December, 1971, of a committee called the Citizens' Crusade Against Crime. At a press conference at City Hall, the three men announced that the committee would assign representatives to follow Presidential candidates around the country and compel them to address themselves to "America's number-one problem—crime and violence." Their announcement came only a few days after Mayor John Lindsay had announced his Presidential candidacy. "Today we hang the albatross of violent crime around the neck of Mayor Lindsay," they said. But they emphasized that they would also try to hang it around the necks of all other candidates. Schneider said he hoped to enlist in the "crusade" many of the five thousand persons who had written him. At this writing, it is too early to tell how much success, if any, the "crusade" will have in preventing crime in Hunts Point or anywhere else.

Just what can be done to curb the seemingly perpetual crime wave in Hunts Point? What is being done now, other than the formation of the Citizens' Crusade Against Crime? Some of the answers can be found in a small, cluttered room on the ground floor of the 41st Precinct station house on Simpson Street. The room is the headquarters of the precinct's Community Relations Unit. Although the unit is small —made up of only two officers—its work is considered a key element in attempts to reduce crime in Hunts Point. Its main duty is to improve the strained relations between the police and the public in the area, opening lines of communication and fostering mutual cooperation.

The commanding officer of the unit is George Garcia, forty-two, a veteran of nineteen years on the police force. A chunky, soft-spoken man, he has served in the Community Relations Unit for six of the seven years of its existence. Garcia's assistant, Wilfred Caban, thirty-three, has spent one of his nine years on the police force in the unit. Both men speak fluent Spanish, a major advantage in dealing with Hunts Point's largely Puerto Rican population.

One of the chief problems in the precinct, Garcia says, is that many Hunts Pointers don't trust the police and view them as "the enemy." These people include thousands of law-abiding citizens who are the victims of the criminal element. Their failure to cooperate with the police increases enormously the law-enforcement problem in the area. Many crimes are not reported to the police, and even if they are investigating officers often find that witnesses refuse to provide any information. Garcia and Caban are trying to break down such resistance and encourage joint efforts by the police and the citizenry against lawlessness.

Their entire emphasis is on gaining the confidence of the community. "We work in civilian clothes," Garcia says. "We try not to get involved in making arrests, unless it's absolutely necessary. Our job is not to arrest people; it's to improve relations between the police and the community."

How do they go about it? For one thing, one or the other of them is on call around the clock to try to settle any legitimate grievance a citizen voices against a policeman. Often, citizen complaints result from misunderstandings. "Lots of times, hostility arises when an officer is not able to communicate with the people on the street," Garcia says. "Let's say a guy is getting arrested for pushing drugs. He's a Puerto Rican and the officer is not. The officer doesn't speak any Spanish. The first thing you know, a big mob of Puerto

Ricans forms on the street and accuses the officer of making an unnecessary arrest. The mob may try to take the prisoner away from the officer. Since the officer can't speak Spanish, he can't explain that the guy is a pusher and that the arrest is necessary. All the mob knows is that a Puerto Rican is being arrested." In such a case, where possible, Garcia or Caban would rush to the scene at the time of the disturbance and try to make clear to the mob why the arrest was both justified and necessary. If one of them could not arrive during the actual disturbance, he would go to the area later and explain the circumstances to the residents.

The two officers also attend numerous meetings with community groups to try to iron out potential problems between the police and the citizenry. "It used to be that some group or other was constantly picketing the precinct house, protesting against treatment by the police," Garcia says. "You could never walk in the door without going through a picket line. Now, we try to find out about problems and solve them before they reach the protest stage. Once in a while we still get some picketing. But even then, the group involved usually calls me and warns me in advance what it's all about. Most of the time the thing can be settled without blowing up into a major problem."

At their meetings with community groups, Garcia and Caban emphasize that effective law enforcement is a two-way street between the police and the public. "We try to point out not only what the police can do to help the community but what the community can do for the police," Garcia says. One way in which Garcia and Caban enlist the help of the public is by seeking the active cooperation of citizens in identifying Hunts Point drug pushers and addicts.

The two officers distribute throughout the community mimeographed notices, printed in English and Spanish, that carry the following message:

Narcotics pushers are blood-suckers, draining the life's blood out of our young, making prostitutes, pimps, and thieves out of children before they have a chance to grow up. This is everyone's problem, not just a police problem. The police need your help in combating this problem.

Anyone having knowledge of drug addicts and drug pushers is asked to please convey this information to the local police precinct or call 911 (the police emergency telephone number). If you do not wish to give your name and address, we will respect your wishes. Whenever possible, give as much information as possible regarding the suspected person or location.

The notices ask citizens to provide the 41st Precinct with such information on narcotics suspects as their names, addresses, approximate ages, physical descriptions, automobile license numbers, and accomplices' identities. While the idea of turning police informer is alien to many Hunts Pointers, the program is nonetheless achieving partial success. Some citizens, although they may distrust the police, are swayed by the realization that the chief threat to their safety comes from narcotics users. In the hope of weakening the criminal element's stranglehold on Hunts Point, they provide the police with the requested tips on drug pushers and addicts. Many other citizens, however, refuse to help the police in any way.

The enormity of the drug problem in Hunts Point is staggering. On some streets—such as Simpson, Fox, and Tiffany —it is estimated that at least one resident out of five uses heroin and that one out of every four youths between the ages of seven and twenty has an arrest record. "If we could eliminate narcotics, we could eliminate at least sixty percent of all crime in this precinct," Garcia says. But he recognizes that the chances of doing so in the foreseeable future are virtually nonexistent.

Garcia and Caban seek the public's help not only in fighting the narcotics problem, but also in combating all other forms of crime that plague Hunts Point. "Many times crimes are committed and the victims refuse to come in and sign complaints," Garcia says. "They say they don't have the time. Some of them have had bad experiences in the past. Maybe they've signed a complaint and then they've had to take a day off from work to show up in court when the case is called for trial. Then the case is postponed, so they have to take another day off when it's called again. Often there's one postponement after another. Naturally, if a complainant is losing a day's pay every time a case is postponed, he's going to be leery about ever signing a complaint again—particularly when he lives in a neighborhood like this and every penny counts. Another problem in this precinct is that many of the crimes don't even get reported to the police. A lot of these crimes are burglaries committed by junkies. The victims figure the chances of an arrest or recovery of the stolen property are practically nil. They say things like: 'If I report it, what'll the cops do? Take my name and address—that's all.' Well, we go out into the community and try to persuade the people that they've got to cooperate with the police if they want to cut down on crime. They've got to report crimes to the police; they've got to sign complaints; they've got to show up in court as witnesses. Otherwise, we're never going to make a dent in the crime problem here. It's tough going, but we're making progress."

Some of this progress is attributable to an organization designed to foster cooperation between the public and the police in Hunts Point. The organization, made up of both private citizens and policemen, is called the 41st Precinct Community Council. Its president is a physician, Dr. Richard Izquierdo, who heads a community health center on Southern Boulevard. "We ask people in the community to serve as representatives on the community council," Garcia says. "We try to get two or three representatives from every block in the precinct." At community council meetings, attempts are made to resolve problems arising between citizens and policemen and to arrange more effective police protection.

One of the complaints frequently voiced at such meetings is that "you can never find a cop when you need one." The police concede that the complaint, while perhaps overstated, has some foundation. For the 41st Precinct, the area with the most serious crime problem in New York City, has an estimated 161,000 persons packed into its two and a half square miles and fewer than 400 policemen to protect them. Taking into account days off, vacations, and the fact that the precinct force is divided into three eight-hour shifts a day, fewer than 100 officers are usually on duty at any one time. Thus, for every policeman on duty, there are more than 1,600 Hunts Pointers needing protection.

With that sort of ratio between policemen and citizens in a high-crime area, residents' complaints about the scarcity of protection seem justified. "One of the problems we have is that our officers often get tied up on petty things that take up an awful lot of time," Caban says. "Let's say a radio car is assigned to investigate a report of a family fight. Most of the time, these are minor incidents. But the officers have to go out and check on them. Maybe it's a case that shouldn't take the officers more than five minutes or so to settle. But they find everybody screaming at everybody else, one things leads to another, and they have to spend thirty or forty minutes out of their car. Well, for that thirty or forty minutes, they're not available to handle more important cases. But the family fights can't be ignored; once in a while they lead to really serious violence."

Through the community council, Garcia and Caban try to explain to Hunts Point residents the problems faced by the police and to persuade them that the police are making genuine efforts to reduce crime in the area. They also use the community council as a vehicle for demonstrating that the police sincerely want to work with the citizenry in improving the general quality of life in Hunts Point.

"We've started a whole bunch of youth programs under the community council to try to show the kids in this area that we're not their enemies," Garcia says. "Every year, we have a Christmas party for about eight hundred kids. The community council asks businessmen in the neighborhood to donate gifts. For many of these poor kids, these are the only Christmas presents they'll get. Actually, eight hundred kids are not very many; there are about twenty-seven thousand school children in this precinct. But we're doing the best we can. We also have a bowling program for the kids. We take them to a bowling alley on Saturdays and get them started. Many of them have never seen the inside of a bowling alley before. Even if they just bowl one or two lines, it's a beginning. Policemen come in on their off-duty time to coach the kids. It's a way of showing that cops *do* care about these kids.

"Awhile back, we found out that the Black Panthers and the Young Lords [a militant Puerto Rican organization] were giving kids in the neighborhood lessons on how to use karate on cops. We decided to use some reverse psychology; we'd set up our own physical fitness course and let the cops teach karate and boxing to the kids. Of course, we're not teaching them how to attack anyone else; we're stressing that these maneuvers should be used only in self-defense. We've got a patrolman named James McLaughlin, who holds a black belt in karate, heading the program. It's been very popular. There are about two hundred kids taking the course."

With the help of the community council, Garcia and Caban are also working with Hunts Point youth gangs—trying to divert their energies from street violence to more constructive channels. "One gang, called the Ghetto Brothers, was having trouble finding a place to meet," Garcia says. "We helped get the gang a storefront to use as a headquarters." By establishing liaison with the gangs, Garcia and Caban feel they are able to reduce the likelihood of violent confrontations in the streets. Occasionally they get advance word that a rumble is scheduled to take place between two rival gangs. They sometimes are able to intercede and mediate the dispute, thus heading off the rumble.

Despite the many constructive steps taken by Garcia, Caban, and other policemen in the 41st Precinct, they harbor no illusions that the corner has been turned in solving Hunts Point's pervasive crime problems. "All you have to do is walk out on the street and you can see the evidence of crime all around you," Garcia says. "Within a few blocks of the station house, walking along the street, you can see maybe four hundred junkies. Right up the street here, a half a block away at the corner of Simpson Street and Westchester Avenue, is the biggest congregation of prostitutes in the area. Some of them are girls as young as seventeen. All of them are junkies. We know how serious the crime problem is in this precinct. We've made a start in fighting it. But we've still got a hell of a long way to go!"

7

"With all the other problems in Hunts Point—it may sound strange to say this —but one of the biggest underlying problems here is that the people have no sense of belonging anywhere," says Mrs. Rita Owens, a social worker. "To them, Hunts Point is nothing but a miserable, filthy ghetto, so they don't think in terms of belonging here. If you ask them where they're from, they never say 'Hunts Point.' They say 'Puerto Rico' or 'South Carolina' or 'Georgia' or wherever else they used to live. They never even consider that Hunts Point may have been a beautiful place once or that it can ever be beautiful again. They just assume that it's always been a slum and always will be one, so the thing they want most is to get away from it. There's no feeling of continuity—of wanting to sink roots here. The people know nothing about Hunts Point's history. I'll bet you could stop twenty people on the street and ask them why this area is called Hunts Point and not one of them would know. I confess I don't know myself."

Mrs. Owens' theory was put to the test. Twenty persons, chosen at random, were stopped on Hunts Point Avenue and asked whether they knew how Hunts Point got its name. Not one knew the answer. Nor did any of the twenty know anything about the history of Hunts Point.

Anyone sufficiently curious to do a bit of research will find that Hunts Point actually has had a long and rich history. Its sons played prominent roles in the formation of the United States, in the Revolutionary War, and in this nation's succeeding wars. Its soil echoed to the boots of George Washington's troops. In short, it was a place where people could be proud to belong.

Before the first white men arrived on the scene, Hunts Point was occupied by various Indian tribes whose territories shifted from time to time. The Indians called the area Quinnahung. The first white settlers were two English colonists, Edward Jessup and John Richardson. On March 12, 1663, they bought the Indian rights to a large tract of land that included Quinnahung. Jessup and Richardson actually took possession of the land three years later, on April 25, 1666, by obtaining a grant from the British colonial government of New York. The grant, which later came to be called the West Farms Patent, included land along the west bank of the Bronx River (then known by the Indian name Ahquahung) —running from what is now the Fordham section of the Bronx south to the East River and west to a small brook called Sackwrahung that followed a course along what is now Intervale Avenue. From this property, Jessup and Richardson set aside two home plots—each consisting of thirty acres of upland and eight acres of meadow—near what is now the intersection of Hunts Point and Lafayette Avenues.

Not much is known about Richardson, but there is a considerable amount of information available on Jessup. From all accounts, he was regarded as one of the most distinguished New York colonists of his time. Although he sprang from an illustrious English family, Jessup had little sympathy for the privileged ruling class of the mother country. He was an ardent champion of the colonists' rights in relation to the Crown.

In 1665 Jessup was a leading delegate to the Convention of Towns in Hempstead, Long Island—the first representative deliberative body ever to assemble in New York. He spoke out forcefully at the convention on behalf of the people's right to choose their own magistrates, instead of having them appointed by the King. Later, Jessup himself was chosen as a magistrate. He was also the founder of a distinguished American family that included, among others, Major General Thomas Sidney Jessup, a hero of the War of 1812 and the Mexican War who was regarded several times as a prominent contender for the Democratic Presidential nomination.

Edward Jessup had a daughter named Elizabeth who married a wealthy young man named Thomas Hunt, Jr. When Jessup died, his land passed into the hands of Hunt. The section originally called Quinnahung by that time was known as Planting Neck. But during Hunt's ownership, it was given the name Hunts Point—and that name has stuck ever since. The word "Point" in the name refers to the tip of land at the south end of the area, jutting into the junction of the Bronx and East Rivers. Although the name was used originally to describe only the property in fairly close proximity to the actual "Point," it has been applied over the years to an area stretching considerably farther inland.

Thomas Hunt, Jr., and John Richardson cultivated everwidening sections of Hunts Point, and began selling parcels of land to other colonists. Dozens of new houses sprang up in the area. In 1669, Hunt sold his home lot and built a house in another section of Hunts Point near what is now Barretto Street. Nineteen years later the Hunt family erected a magnificent mansion nearby, called The Grange.

When Hunt died, the family property was taken over by his oldest son, Thomas Hunt III. He expanded his holdings in 1700 by acquiring all of Richardson's property in Hunts Point. The combined Hunt-Richardson property remained in the Hunt family through the middle of the nineteenth century. By 1760, ownership of The Grange and the family's

[73]

other holdings had passed into the hands of the original Hunt's grandson, Thomas Hunt IV. In the tradition of the earlier owner of the property, Edward Jessup, Thomas Hunt IV was an outspoken advocate of colonial rights.

During the Revolution, Hunt became a prominent leader of the colonial forces in New York and a close friend and confidant of George Washington. He was instrumental in organizing several companies of Minutemen. And he served as an influential member of the New York Committee of Safety, which carried on the functions of government during the transition period between the overthrow of the British colonial governor and the creation of a state government.

In retaliation for Hunt's activism on the colonial side, the British fleet ordered a frigate named the *Asia* to sail up the East River to a point near The Grange and bombard the mansion and its surrounding estate with cannons. The attack forced Hunt and his family to flee temporarily from the estate. They returned later to find the mansion damaged, but still standing. Some of the cannonballs fired by the British remained embedded in the mansion's walls until the early 1900's.

When Washington's troops were forced to retreat from the British in the Battle of Long Island, they fled by boat across the East River and then trudged through Hunts Point along an old colonial road near the west bank of the Bronx River. The pursuing British made their way along the river's east bank. Washington's men were in disarray as a result of the Long Island defeat, but were able to regroup while in Hunts Point. They fought a delaying action as they moved north, trading shots across the river with the British. (One can only speculate how much more exciting might have been the street games played along "The Creek" by later generations of Hunts Point children—ignorant of the area's history—if they had just known that Washington and his troops had once engaged the enemy there.) The northward course of the two armies eventually led to a major battle at White Plains. Although British General William Howe's troops won the battle, they failed to accomplish their main objective—the destruction of Washington's army. Some historians believe much more dire consequences would have befallen Washington's men if they had not been able to reorganize their forces at Hunts Point.

The small cemetery at Hunts Point and Oak Point Avenues, where poet Joseph Rodman Drake is buried, also contains the graves of a number of soldiers killed during the Revolution. Drake, a friend of various members of the Hunt family, lived at The Grange for the final years of his life. He was only twenty-five when he died of consumption on September 21, 1820. Buried near Drake in the cemetery are several generations of the Hunt family and other settlers of Hunts Point. Opposite the Hunt family plot is a small enclosure containing the graves of Negro slaves owned by the area's early residents.

In 1824, the Marquis de Lafayette, making a heralded tour of the United States, visited Hunts Point and paid tribute to the roles played in the Revolution by Thomas Hunt IV and other Hunts Pointers. He paused in silent meditation at the graves of members of the Hunt family, Joseph Rodman Drake, and the Revolutionary soldiers buried in the cemetery. After leaving the cemetery, he passed through a narrow lane that was later widened and named Lafayette Avenue in his honor.

As the years passed, most of the reminders of Hunts Point's colonial history disappeared. The old homes were torn down, the estates were carved up into smaller parcels, the pioneer families died out or moved away, and thousands of new residents settled in the area. By 1908, when Mrs. Kathleen Wiener moved into Irvine Street, one of the few relics remaining was The Grange. The old mansion still stood majestically overlooking the East River—a tribute to the glories of the past. But age eventually caught up with The Grange. Within another decade it, too, was gone.

Throughout its history, Hunts Point has continued to produce men who have made their marks in the world of politics and government. One of the most beloved public servants to come out of Hunts Point during the twentieth century was a distinguished Bronx County judge, Harry Stackell, who served on the bench for decades. For years, an annual award for high character was given in Judge Stackell's honor to a student at P.S. 48. In 1965, after the judge's retirement from the bench, a visitor noted that he spent much of his time reading the Bible, and asked why. Stackell, then past the age of eighty, replied: "I'm reading the Bible because I'm cramming for the finals." Stackell died on January 19, 1972, at the age of eighty-eight.

In Congress, most of Hunts Point currently is represented by James H. Scheuer, a Democrat with a liberal voting record. A small sliver of Hunts Point lies within the district of Congressman Herman Badillo, a Puerto Rican with a tremendous following among members of minority groups, both in the Bronx and elsewhere. Badillo, a former Bronx borough president who is becoming increasingly influential on the national political scene, is idolized by many young Hunts Pointers. On his frequent visits to Hunts Point, he is trailed through the streets by scores of cheering teen-agers.

In 1971, a Hunts Pointer took over a job tantamount to being Puerto Rico's ambassador to the mainland United States. Nick Lugo, Jr., who grew up on Kelly Street, was appointed at the age of twenty-eight as national executive director of the Commonwealth of Puerto Rico's Migration Division. During Lugo's childhood, his father—a native Puerto Rican and a leader in the movement to obtain statehood for the island—founded a travel and insurance agency on Westchester Avenue in Hunts Point. After his graduation from high school in the Bronx, the younger Lugo attended the Inter-American University in Puerto Rico, then returned to Hunts Point to take a managerial job in his father's business. The business flourished, establishing branch offices throughout the New York metropolitan area. It also set up subsidiaries to operate finance, real estate, and travel agencies in San Juan. Young Lugo's talent in supervising the Puerto Rican subsidiaries brought him to the attention of Puerto Rico's governor, Luis A. Ferre, who appointed him to the Migration Division job. Lugo thus became the youngest head of an executive department in the Puerto Rican government.

While success stories such as those of Nick Lugo and Herman Badillo might be expected to inspire Hunts Point youngsters to dream of pulling themselves out of the ghetto, this is only rarely the case. More often, these youngsters see themselves as doomed to lives of deprivation and frustration in Hunts Point or some other slum. Their attitude of despair was summarized by Robert Oliver, a seventeen-year-old Negro high school dropout who was encountered one day as he wandered through the old Hunts Point cemetery—killing time.

"Sure, I think Herman Badillo's a great man," he said. "But what's he gonna do for me? Is he gonna get me a job? Shit, no! Is he gonna get me out of the rat-hole where I live? You kiddin' me, man? Nobody ain't gonna help me." Then, changing the subject and pointing to the grave of Joseph Rodman Drake, he said: "You think I give a damn about a famous poet bein' buried here? When I went to P.S. 48, they used to tell us how proud we should be to have our school named for Joseph Rodman Drake—that he was a big man and he was buried right over here. Well, what the hell does Joseph Rodman Drake mean to me? You think I give a damn about soldiers from the Revolution bein' buried here, either? Am I supposed to get a big thrill out of that? Shit, what did they ever do for me?"

He paused and then pointed to the graves of the colonial-era slaves. "Now, those graves mean somethin' to me," he said. "Those were black people who were brought here as slaves and died as slaves. Just like me. I'm a slave, too. And I'm gonna die here as a slave."

3 detention
centers

8

Those who say that Hunts Point is a "forgotten area" of New York often back up their contention by arguing that the neighborhood is a dumping ground for some of the city government's most repugnant facilities. They point, for example, to the locations of the city's detention centers for juveniles in trouble with the law. There are three such centers to serve the entire city—all of which have been described by independent observers as "houses of horror." The two largest centers have been placed by the city in Hunts Point; the third has been placed nearby in an adjoining section of the Bronx.

"How come we have to have these terrible places here?" asks Mrs. Irma Oliveira, who lives within three blocks of the two detention centers in Hunts Point. "This is supposed to be a residential neighborhood. These places don't belong here. You mean to tell me the city couldn't find any place else in the whole five boroughs to put them? Why couldn't they be put on Staten Island, where there's all that open space? I'll tell you why they're here—because the city doesn't give a damn about Hunts Point!"

The largest and most controversial of the three facilities is the Spofford Juvenile Center at 1221 Spofford Avenue, directly up the street from P.S. 48. A massive gray building, Spofford has been the subject of numerous critical investigations over the years. It has a capacity of 284 inmates, boys and girls awaiting disposition of their cases by the courts. Their ages range from seven to sixteen, and they may be charged with acts ranging from truancy and incorrigibility to homicide. Many of them are at Spofford because they cannot get along with their families. Thus, a "difficult" second-grader whose parents cannot seem to handle him may find himself thrown in with a teen-aged killer.

Most inmates stay at Spofford for at least several weeks while their cases are under consideration by the courts. They then are sent back to their families, placed with private agencies, or ordered into state training schools. Often children spend several separate periods at Spofford because of recurring problems. A recent study showed that, during a one-year period, 1,500 youths were admitted to Spofford twice, 873 were admitted three times, 488 four times, and 287 five times.

Frank Sawchuck, head counselor at Spofford, criticizes the system that places youngsters in the institution. "How do little kids from seven to ten years old get sent here?" he asks. "Can you see a little kid like that being a danger to the community?" Sawchuck, who has worked in New York City detention centers for twenty-two years, feels Spofford's over-burdened facilities and inadequate staff combine to make the place unmanageable. "It's just too big an institution," he says. "You can get some kids to start fighting at one end of a corridor and no one knows about it."

Because of low salaries and the danger inherent in the work, Spofford is unable to attract and keep skilled counselors and social workers. On the average, a case worker stays only eighteen months. At Spofford, he starts at a salary of $7,500 a year. If he worked for other city agencies, he might make from $8,000 to $10,660.

Thus, during one recent period, eight of Spofford's eleven case worker jobs were unfilled, as were seven of the ten recreation counselor jobs. Almost a third of the institution's employees quit every year. If the employees don't like Spofford—and they don't—the inmates like it even less. They complain of brutality by both employees and fellow inmates, of racial disturbances, of drug use, of homosexual assaults, and of generally intolerable conditions.

One fourteen-year-old inmate named John showed an interviewer scars on his arm that he said were knife wounds sustained in a racial fight in Spofford's dining room. A sixteen-year-old named Ernest, confined for a drug offense, said he was able to continue using narcotics in the institution because "they smuggle pills in here sometimes." Other inmates told of being slapped on the side of the head for minor infractions and of being unable to use toilets at night because they were locked in their rooms. A fifteen-year-old named Gary said he was sent to Spofford after being arrested for standing near a stolen car. "I wish the cop would have just smashed me instead of putting me here," Gary said. "I just think about home all the time." On visiting days, Gary's parents stay home in Brooklyn with their nine other children. "They don't like to come here," he said. "They think there are a bunch of bad kids here."

One of the many investigations of conditions at Spofford was launched in November, 1970, after the death of a fourteen-year-old inmate. The youth, Victor Negron, died of serum hepatitis—apparently the result of using narcotics. Yet Spofford officials said they had considered him in good health until shortly before his death, and had received no indication he was a drug user.

New York City Councilman Robert Postel, a vocal critic of the Spofford authorities, blamed them for young Negron's death. "He died not from hepatitis, as hospital authorities will tell you," Postel said. "He died because of criminal neglect on the part of administrators at Spofford. Victor Negron came to Spofford on November 11. At that time, he was suffering from hepatitis. He grew so weak over the course of the days he spent at Spofford that his young dormitory mates had to carry him from activity to activity. He didn't eat for days. The children in that dorm have reported that they saw his face grow dark and his eyes become a deepening yellow."

Postel said Negron asked to be admitted to Spofford's infirmary, but that the request was denied. "The boy went back to his dormitory after he was refused treatment," the councilman said. "He told his fellow children: 'I'm dying. They won't let me in because they don't have enough beds.'" On November 20, two days after he had been denied admission to the infirmary, Negron's condition had become sufficiently serious that Spofford officials sent him to an outside hospital. He died at the hospital on November 25.

John A. Wallace, director of probation in the New York City Office of Probation, which operates Spofford, said Negron was found to be in good health when he was admitted to the detention center. "He had no known history of drug abuse," Wallace said. But he conceded that, after the youth's death, Spofford officials learned Negron had told other inmates he used drugs.

Councilman Postel, calling Spofford "the most barbaric and inhumane place in the city of New York," demanded the dismissal of the institution's top administrators. He also called for the administration of the three city youth shelters to be taken away from the Office of Probation and turned over to a proposed City Department of Institutional Child Care. Lashing out at both Spofford's medical personnel and chief administrators, the councilman said: "I believe very truthfully that they are incompetent. The administrators of the Spofford Juvenile Center have violated ninety-five percent of all state laws governing child-care institutions. Homosexual abuse is widespread there; narcotics are smuggled into the institution; children are forced to sleep on vomit-encrusted sheets and urine-soaked mattresses that other children slept on the night before."

Bronx District Attorney Burton B. Roberts, partly in response to Postel's charges of criminal neglect, launched an investigation into Negron's death and into general conditions at Spofford. A month later, he announced that the investigation had turned up no evidence worthy of being referred to a grand jury. Roberts said the inquiry into Negron's death "showed a complete lack of criminal negligence on the part of anyone connected with it."

Undaunted, Councilman Postel kept up a steady drumfire of criticism of Spofford officials. He charged that conditions at the center were so poor that four youths had tried to commit suicide during one ten-day period. "Are these suicide attempts not proof enough of barbaric conditions at Spofford and the dire need for reform there?" he asked. "Or must we wait for the death of another child to shock us into action?"

Wallace Nottage, the city's deputy director of probation in charge of institutional services, acknowledged that "We've had a rash" of suicide attempts at Spofford—but he preferred to call them "suicide gestures." He claimed: "Kids have been heard to say, 'If you want to get out of here, all you have to do is cut your wrists.'"

While the controversy over Negron's death and the attempted suicides was still raging, a new uproar arose over the discovery of a heroin cache inside Spofford. It was found that a fifteen-year-old inmate had smuggled eighty bags of heroin, a hypodermic needle, and a syringe into the institution. The contraband had been sewn into the lining of his clothing when he had been admitted. By the time of the discovery, all but three of the bags had been used by the youngster and his fellow inmates. The youth, who had been taking heroin since the age of ten, had been sent to Spofford on a narcotics charge. Yet he had apparently been given only a cursory search when he'd entered. A detective from District Attorney Roberts' office, assigned to Spofford at the request of institutional authorities, had uncovered the remaining heroin.

Roberts also assigned a second detective to work undercover at Spofford as a counselor—looking for further evidence of drug use. The undercover man, Alan Brenner, said he discovered within three weeks that another counselor, named Watson Hickson, was selling heroin. Brenner made a "buy" of twenty-eight bags of heroin from Hickson, he said, followed by a purchase of fifteen additional bags. After the second "buy," Hickson was arrested and charged with possession and sale of drugs.

Meanwhile, there was a sharp increase in the volume and intensity of public criticism aimed at both Spofford and its supervising officials. Former U.S. Supreme Court Justice Arthur Goldberg was one of many critics. After visiting the institution, Goldberg accused officials of tolerating "widespread violence, drug abuse, and homosexuality."

A short time later the Institute for Juvenile Justice, a national organization seeking to protect the interests of children, announced plans to take court action to close Spofford "once and for all." The organization's director, Lawrence Cole, called the institution a "house of horrors." At a news conference, he produced a thirteen-year-old boy who had been sent to Spofford for running away from home. The boy said he had been repeatedly beaten by guards and subjected to other abuses. The Institute for Juvenile Justice filed a petition for writs of *habeas corpus* on behalf of about half of Spofford's inmates—claiming they were being held illegally either because they had been held for more than three days without court hearings or had been held for more than forty-five days after hearings. Later, the institute pressed in court for complete shutdown of the center. But, at this writing, neither court action has produced tangible results.

The second juvenile detention center in Hunts Point is the

Manida Center, at 765 Manida Street, which houses about seventy girls between the ages of seven and sixteen. Although it takes a back seat to Spofford in the notoriety department, Manida has been the focus of its own share of controversy. In December, 1970, for example, a Manida counselor was kicked in the face by an inmate, and the incident resulted in a brief strike by the 278 counselors at all three detention centers. They claimed the attack could have been prevented if the kicked victim had been accompanied by another counselor, but that there was a severe shortage of counselors because of a city job freeze ordered by Mayor Lindsay. They insisted they would not return to their jobs until the city lifted the freeze on hiring detention center workers and provided two counselors for each dormitory.

The walkout caused great consternation in Hunts Point. Neighborhood residents, who didn't like the centers in their midst in the first place, were aghast at the idea of the inmates being left without adequate supervision. They had visions of mass escapes and wild rampages through the streets by the inmates. As a precaution, police details were stationed outside the three detention centers. But inside, only handfuls of supervisory employees were on duty. Recognizing the situation was volatile, city officials quickly capitulated to the demands and the strike ended. But other events later contrived to keep Manida in the spotlight.

On September 29, 1971, two Manida employees were arrested on charges of trying to enlist women to engage in prostitution. One defendant, the Reverend Louis A. Holliday, was a forty-six-year-old minister who served simultaneously as a counselor at Manida and as pastor of the Soundview Avenue Baptist Church in the Bronx. The other defendant was Miss Sarah Cole, forty-three, who also held down two jobs—one as a Manida counselor and the other as Holliday's secretary at the church. They were taken into custody at Miss Cole's Bronx apartment after detectives had tailed them from a street corner on the Upper West Side of Manhattan. The detectives accused them of trying to solicit two married women to engage in prostitution. A prosecutor said the investigation leading to the arrests had been in progress for almost two months.

Although the specific charges filed against Holliday and Miss Cole did not relate directly to their duties at Manida, the arrests nonetheless created a new furor at the detention center. How was the center supposed to help rehabilitate delinquent girls, critics asked, if it employed persons involved in prostitution? Didn't this incident lead to the unavoidable conclusion that background checks made on prospective Manida employees must have been inadequate? Moreover, why were Holliday and Miss Cole allowed to continue serving as counselors during the two-month period in which they were under investigation? True, they were not charged with any crime until the end of that period. But couldn't some way have been found to prevent them from dealing with Manida's young girls once they became suspect, without either violating their rights or jeopardizing the pending investigation? To all such questions, there were no immediate answers from the authorities.

Meanwhile, the authorities at all three detention centers and the institutions themselves were subjected to a continuing barrage of criticism. A special eighteen-member task force appointed by the Citizens Committee for Children of New York urged after a year-long study that Spofford, Manida, and the third institution, the Zerega Juvenile Center, be "closed or converted to other uses with reasonable speed." The task force charged that conditions at the three centers were so "appalling" that the institutions were "often destructive of the children for whom they are maintained."

Mrs. John A. Willis, chairman of the task force, called the plight of the children held in the centers "deplorable." Her group's written report assailed not only the specific conditions at Spofford, Manida, and Zerega, but also the entire concept of maintaining such large detention centers. Merely closing down the three institutions and erecting new ones to take their places would be self-defeating, the task force said. It advocated a broad-scale reform of the whole system for dealing with children in need of supervision.

"The relatively few children found to be a potential danger to the community or themselves should be placed in small, secure detention residences reasonably close to the courts," the report said. "Other children should be placed in very small residential and nonresidential services in the neighborhoods, including foster homes and day centers. We get what we give in this world. And, if we do not improve conditions for these children, we will get compassionless, alienated, brutal adults who are the logical end of our work."

Since the task force was merely an unofficial body of concerned citizens, its report and recommendations were not binding on public officials. Its main hope was to focus public attention on the need for reform and thus spur governmental action. To an extent, this hope was realized. The Appellate Division of New York State Supreme Court, responsible for overseeing operation of the three centers by the City Office of Probation, appointed a panel to conduct its own *official* investigation. The panel, headed by Judge Joseph Stone of the New York City Criminal Court, made a six-month inquiry and issued an eighty-seven-page report highly critical of the centers. It recommended a major overhaul of the entire system for handling juvenile offenders in the city. Among other things, the panel urged that both Manida and Zerega be closed immediately because "both these facilities are in such deplorable condition as to constitute a serious danger and hazard to the health and safety of the occupants."

Although the panel found many serious problems at Spofford as well, it did not recommend the closing of that center. But it did urge that Spofford be used to house only those children who seemed to require confinement in a maximum-security institution. To replace Manida and Zerega and to accommodate those children from Spofford who didn't need maximum-security facilities, the panel urged construction of new, non-secure centers elsewhere in the city and small, secure centers in close proximity to the courts. It also recommended broad-scale reform of the measures employed at the institutions—saying children had suffered physical abuse at the hands of staff members, that medical procedures were inadequate, and that the schooling provided inmates was sporadic and ineffective.

The panel's report was generally praised, with Mayor Lindsay calling it an "excellent and important document." The mayor said an extensive investigation would be launched to determine what action should be taken on the findings. Some critics complained that there had already been enough investigations—that the time had come to act—but Lindsay insisted that further study was needed to decide how to implement the panel's recommendations.

Several months later, the mayor announced the city would soon open two non-secure residential facilities in neighborhood settings for juveniles charged with minor crimes or considered in need of supervision. His plan called for removing some of the younger children from Spofford and placing them in the new facilities, which would house about twenty-five youngsters each. In addition, Lindsay said, the new residences would facilitate the eventual closing of Manida and Zerega. The key word, however, was "eventual." Although the court-appointed panel had urged the immediate closing of Manida and Zerega, its recommendation had not been followed.

In early 1972, subordinates of Lindsay disclosed they were developing plans that went far beyond the two non-secure residential facilities. These embryonic plans provided for ten to twenty juvenile reception centers, plus up to forty homes in each of which eight to twelve children would live with "house parents," adult couples, in settings approximating home life. Under this plan, officials "hope" Manida can be phased out of existence in a year and Zerega in eighteen to twenty months. They also "hope" Spofford—which the court-appointed panel had recommended stay open—can be phased out in about five years. It should be emphasized, however, that these are merely plans formulated by city agencies and have not even been approved by the mayor at this point—much less by other branches of government such as the city council and board of estimate. And there is no guarantee they will be.

Whether city officials would be able to persuade various neighborhoods to accept the new facilities is far from certain. Certainly, recent events make it obvious that residents of other neighborhoods are no more anxious than Hunts Pointers to have such institutions in their midst.

When the city proposed to place one of the non-secure facilities approved by Lindsay in a residential area of the Bronx near the huge Parkchester housing development, a storm of protest arose. The plan called for the facility to be situated on Beach Avenue, across the street from the Blessed Sacrament Roman Catholic Church and parochial school. At a hearing called by city officials to explain their plan to local residents, leaders and members of the church and school insisted they would not accept the facility in their neighborhood. After a heated session, the spokesman for the City Office of Probation, David Schwartz, threw up his hands and asked: "What neighborhood is going to want this?"

What neighborhood indeed! The residents in the Parkchester area didn't want it. Hunts Pointers didn't want it. And it would be fair to assume that no other neighborhood in the city would want it, either. The difference between Parkchester and Hunts Point, however, appeared to be that residents of the Parkchester area had some political leverage.

They weren't ghetto residents. They were middle-class New Yorkers. Thus, while Hunts Pointers were stuck at least for the immediate future with Spofford and Manida, those in Parkchester quickly won concessions from the city. Officials of the Office of Probation changed their original plan to provide that no youths charged with criminal offenses—only boys from ten to sixteen who were either truants or runaways —would be kept at the proposed Beach Avenue facility. Even then, local residents continued their opposition—although the area's community planning board did approve the project. At this writing, the institution's fate is uncertain. But, at worst, the Parkchester residents will be saddled with a facility whose inmates will be considered far less "dangerous" than those at Spofford and Manida.

"You think the city would have paid that much attention to the protest if people in Hunts Point were doing the screaming, instead of people up there around Parkchester?" asks a Hunts Pointer, Benjamin Williams. "Bullshit! If it was us, they'd have shoved it down our throats!"

Certain observers wonder why Hunts Pointers object so strongly to the location of centers such as Spofford and Manida in their neighborhood. After all, they argue, these facilities generally should not cause any disruption of the lives of local residents. Their problems—severe as they are— usually do not overflow beyond the walls of the institutions. The centers, these observers contend, might even afford employment opportunities that would otherwise not be available to people living in the area.

To all of this, many Hunts Pointers respond with derisive laughs. "Listen, we got enough problems in this area without needing those places," says a typical resident, Mrs. Carmela Sanchez, who lives a block away from Spofford. "Suppose a bunch of those kids escape and start tearing up the neighborhood or taking hostages. You think I want my kids or my husband or myself exposed to something like that? Why should we have to be the ones right next door to these places? You don't see the people in fancy neighborhoods in Manhattan getting stuck with this kind of problem. Why should we?"

Another Hunts Pointer, Bernard Oliver, echoes Mrs. Sanchez's sentiments. "Look, on visiting days we got relatives of juvenile delinquents from all over the city coming into Hunts Point," he says. "Many of these people are criminals themselves. They're pissed off when they get here because their kids or brothers or sisters are bein' held in these miserable places. Sometimes, they take it out on people in the neighborhood—beatin' up on them or robbin' them. It's not that they got anythin' personal against the people around here. They're just pissed off and they take it out on anyone they see. Well, man, who needs that kind of crap? There's enough trouble in Hunts Point caused by the people who live here; we don't need no more from outsiders."

As for the contention that the juvenile centers might provide jobs for Hunts Pointers, Oliver says: "It don't work out that way. The people hired there need a certain amount of education and so forth that most of us in this neighborhood don't have. They're gettin' their employees from all over the city—not from Hunts Point. I don't know one person from this neighborhood who works at Spofford or Manida. It's not like this was a town like Ossining, where Sing Sing is. There, the prison helps the whole town's economy. Most of the prison workers live in the town or nearby. But here, hell, these centers get their workers from just about everywhere except Hunts Point. We get all the disadvantages of havin' the places in our neighborhood, but we don't get any of the advantages."

Another city-operated facility that has generated frequent complaints from neighborhood residents is the Hunts Point Terminal Market. Situated on a vast tract on the west bank of the Bronx River near the southern end of the Hunts Point area, the market serves as New York's main distribution center for produce and certain other foods. Although operated by the city, it is occupied by private firms—most of them large wholesale food distributors. It was built by the city during the 1960's to replace the old Washington Street market in Lower Manhattan. During the planning and construction stages, city officials forecast that the opening of the new market would bring an economic resurgence to the depressed area—providing jobs to Hunts Point's unemployed, additional business to neighborhood residents, and assorted other blessings.

That rosy outlook, however, has not been borne out by events. By and large, as in the case of the juvenile centers, those employed at the market are not Hunts Pointers. Many of the workers, who reside throughout the New York metropolitan area, had previously been employed by various produce wholesalers at the old Washington Street market. When the employers moved to the Hunts Point market, the workers simply went along with them. Thus, no vast supply of job opportunities was opened to Hunts Pointers. Since they had been led to believe otherwise, local residents were understandably embittered. Moreover, with a few exceptions, Hunts Point merchants did not benefit substantially from the opening of the market, either. Luncheonettes and diners picked up additional business, but most other establishments reported no significant gains. Generally, the people who worked at the market did their shopping near their residences —in most cases, far from Hunts Point. Thus, even with the market operating at full capacity, unemployment among Hunts Point residents remained three times as high as the national average.

Neighborhood residents complain that the market has brought new problems to the already troubled area, but has not brought the promised benefits. "Those huge tractor-trailer trucks come tearing through the neighborhood, on their way to and from the market, at all hours of the day and night," says Mrs. Hortensia Gotay. "They're so loud they can wake the dead. It's impossible to get a decent night's sleep around here because of all the noise. And when our kids are out on the street, we're scared to death that they'll be run down by one of these trucks. The drivers drive like maniacs. They act like they don't care who gets in their way; they just want to get through with their work as quick as they can."

Another reason for resentment of the market is that it has added substantially to the already critical crime problem in Hunts Point. The market has become a magnet for drug pushers, prostitutes, and thieves. While many of them undoubtedly are members of Hunts Point's own criminal element, local residents contend that many others are drawn to the market from widely scattered sections of New York. Marvin Evans, who lives a few blocks from the market, sounds a familiar refrain: "We got enough junkies, whores, pimps, and thieves of our own. We sure as hell don't need any new ones from Harlem or Brooklyn or somewhere like that."

Underscoring the crime problem at the market was an incident on October 25, 1971, when a policeman was shot and stabbed in a struggle with three men he caught in the act of looting a railroad car filled with produce. Patrolman John F. Scott, a thirty-five-year-old veteran of almost eleven years on the police force, was patrolling the market shortly before dusk when he came upon the looters. He tried to arrest them, but they jumped him, and one of them stabbed him in the right thigh with a knife. In the struggle, Scott's service revolver was taken away from him and one of his assailants then shot him with it, the bullet ripping through his left foot. The looters then fled, taking the officer's gun with them.

Using a walkie-talkie, Scott radioed for assistance: "Help me! I'm shot! Won't somebody please help me?" At the Police Department Communications Bureau, Patrolman Carl

Horn heard the plea and radioed back a request for Scott's position. "I'm lying on a railroad track by a fence in Hunts Point Market," Scott replied. Horn immediately broadcast a signal 1013 alarm, which means "assist policeman."

Thirty-five officers, some of them wearing bullet-proof vests and carrying rifles, rushed to the market. But, with darkness descending, they could not immediately find the wounded patrolman. "We can't locate you," they radioed Scott. "Fire a couple of shots in the air."

"I can't," Scott replied. "They took my gun."

Finally, a radio car from the 41st Precinct found him on a railroad track along a row of the market facing Edgewater Road—a street that runs beside the Bronx River. He was rushed to a hospital, where he eventually recovered. His assailants escaped.

New York City Port and Terminal Commissioner Edgar Baker, whose department operates the market, concedes that a serious crime problem exists there. But he claims he does not know who is primarily responsible—Hunts Pointers or outsiders. No matter who is responsible, the fact remains that local residents are convinced the presence of the market in their community has aggravated their problems and done little to fulfill the promises of city officials that it would greatly benefit the neighborhood.

The residents also complain that the merchants who use the market exploit Hunts Point and have no interest in improving conditions there. They contend, for example, that the merchants pledged to start a fund to be used for improving educational opportunities for local children. The fund supposedly was to serve as a symbol of the merchants' concern for Hunts Point. A fund was started, all right, and $100,000 was reportedly collected. Hunts Pointers charge bitterly, however, that this money was not spent in their neighborhood but was contributed instead for the use of children from more affluent families living in Co-op City—a cooperative apartment house development in another section of the Bronx.

As further evidence of what they consider the city government's indifference to the plight of the average Hunts Pointer—and contrasting concern for special interests such as the merchants at the market—local residents point to the city's snow-removal policy. Whenever there is a heavy snowstorm, the residents maintain, the city gives priority to clearing the market itself and the streets used by trucks in going to and from there. Meanwhile, other streets in Hunts Point—those used primarily by pedestrians and passenger cars—are left cluttered with snow. A case in point was a snowstorm that struck New York in January, 1971. The city sent a special snow-removal force—consisting of about a hundred and twenty men using snow blowers, front-end loaders, thirty dump trucks, and New York's only snow-melting machine—to the market. The men worked in shifts for twenty-three hours to clear the market, while the remainder of Hunts Point was virtually untouched by snow-removal equipment.

City officials contend such special treatment for the market is justified on the ground that the flow of food to New Yorkers must not be interrupted. But many Hunts Pointers ridicule that contention as a handy excuse. "The truth of it is that those people in the market would lose money if any of their merchandise spoiled because the deliveries were held up by the snow," says one local resident, Elvin Tolliver. "So they put pressure on the city to get the market cleared. But we could scream to high heaven and we still wouldn't get the snow cleared off our streets. It sits there for days before the city sends anyone around to remove it. Sometimes, the city never does get around to removing it; it just stays there until it finally melts. It's just another case of Hunts Point getting the shaft. Like everybody says, the city just doesn't give a damn about Hunts Point."

Another sore point with Hunts Pointers is the hospital

service, or lack of it, provided the area by the city. There is no city hospital in Hunts Point, and there never has been. The old Hunts Point Hospital, which was torn down in 1970, was privately owned. Economically deprived Hunts Pointers, unable to afford private hospital care, have been forced for generations to rely on municipally operated Lincoln Hospital. Lincoln, about a mile southwest of Hunts Point at 141st Street and Bruckner Boulevard, has become the focus of heated controversy in recent years.

The hospital is decrepit and overcrowded. Built in 1839 as a nursing home for runaway slaves, and later converted into a hospital, it was condemned three decades ago because of substandard conditions. Yet, it is still in operation today. Although it is the only hospital in an area inhabited by about 400,000 persons—most of them Puerto Ricans and Negroes —it can accommodate only 360 patients. Space is so limited that clinics must be operated in the corridors. There are seemingly interminable waits for X rays and other medical services. An indication of the enormity of the problem is provided by one statistic: Despite its limited facilities, Lincoln's pediatric emergency room alone is called upon to handle about 125,000 cases a year.

Compounding the problem, critics of the hospital charge, has been the insensitivity of the staff to the needs of the area's poverty-stricken residents. Such critics—and they include some members of the staff themselves—accuse the hospital of horrible abuses of accepted medical practice, mistreatment and neglect of patients, and refusal to cooperate with outside groups seeking to improve health conditions in the area.

In protest of conditions at Lincoln, about a hundred and fifty local residents stormed into the five-building hospital complex one summer day in 1970 and seized control of one of the buildings. The demonstrators were led by members of the Young Lords, a militant organization of Puerto Ricans which patterns itself after the Black Panthers, espouses socialism, and which operates from a Bronx headquarters in Hunts Point. Once in control of the building, which contained Lincoln's administrative offices, the Young Lords presented hospital officials with a list of demands for improving health conditions in the area. "We are here with nothing but love for our people," said Pablo Yoruba Guzman, minister of information for the Young Lords. "We are not armed and we will leave this hospital only when it starts serving the people."

Gloria Cruz, who holds the title of health lieutenant in the Young Lords, was more vitriolic. "Lincoln Hospital is only a butcher shop that kills patients and frustrates workers from saving these patients," she said. "This is because Lincoln exists under a capitalist system that only looks for profit. But even this system made an effort at scrapping this butcher shop by condemning this building thirty years ago. . . . The hospital has been taken [by the demonstrators] to release its potential for the benefit of both patients and hospital staff."

Among the demands made by the Young Lords were that the city speed construction of a new hospital to replace Lincoln; that there be no cutbacks in personnel or services at Lincoln despite a city budget crisis; that the city inaugurate a door-to-door preventive care program emphasizing tests for lead poisoning, anemia, tuberculosis, and drug addiction; and that the city provide a day-care center at the hospital for the children of adult out-patients. Representatives of the Young Lords discussed the demands for four hours—while holding the hospital building—with Lincoln Hospital Administrator Antero Lacot, other city health officials, and Sid Davidoff, an assistant to Mayor Lindsay. Dr. Lacot, who had taken over as Lincoln's administrator only six weeks earlier, conceded that the demands were valid. "The Young Lords are trying to dramatize a situation that is critical," Lacot said. "In our hospital we have a lot of needs that have to be taken care of. Because of years and years of neglect we have been suffering, and now we are trying to remedy the situation. We need the cooperation of all segments of the community. We cannot do the job overnight." Although he regarded the dramatization of the hospital's needs as helpful, Lacot said he hoped the Young Lords would leave because their occupation of the building had frightened some Lincoln employees into staying home from work—thus depriving patients of necessary services.

By the time the four-hour negotiating session ended, the demonstrators had occupied the building for twelve hours. Dr. Lacot emerged from the meeting and announced that a tentative agreement had been reached on the demands of the Young Lords. Under the agreement, the demonstrators would leave the building but the Young Lords would later be allowed to run certain health programs at the hospital under the supervision of staff physicians. Further details of the agreement were to be worked out at a meeting scheduled for the following day.

But, before the demonstrators had time to leave the building, a hitch developed. The Young Lords discovered that a policeman, in civilian clothes, had tried to enter the building. The officer had attempted to seize one of the Young Lords stationed at a door of the building to check credentials of those who wanted to enter or leave. Because of the policeman's action, the Young Lords said they were backing out of the agreement and planned to stay in the building and "defend themselves" from the police. A short time later, however, while standing by their refusal to abide by the agreement, the demonstrators decided to leave the building. They hauled down a Puerto Rican flag that they had previously hoisted atop the building, then filed out the doors. Outside, Minister of Information Guzman and his bodyguard, Louis Alvarez Perez, were arrested by the police. Although Guzman had earlier claimed that the demonstrators were not armed, the police charged him and Perez with possession of a dangerous weapon—a pair of chukka sticks, two pieces of wood about eight inches long held together by an elastic thong.

Guzman and Perez were eventually released, but the Young Lords continued their refusal to abide by the tentative agreement. A partial agreement was later reached, however, under which the Young Lords and other activists from the area were permitted to establish a so-called "grievance table" at Lincoln. Patients who had complaints about service received at the hospital would come to the table and state their grievances. If a complaint seemed justified, the activists would try to obtain remedial action by conferring with hospital officials.

Meanwhile, action was being taken by some members of the hospital staff to make Lincoln more responsive to community needs—action that ultimately would lead to still further discord. For years, doctors practicing at Lincoln had complained that the hospital's deplorable conditions made it difficult and sometimes impossible to recruit capable interns and residents who had studied at major American medical schools. The staff was made up chiefly of foreign doctors who had been unable to find jobs at more attractive hospitals. In an attempt both to draw promising young doctors and at the same time try to meet the demands of local residents for greater community control of health care, Lincoln began in 1970 to recruit a new breed of medical school graduate—the "socially conscious and politically aware" intern. It was felt that such idealistic young doctors would come to Lincoln in spite of the poor working conditions in the hope of improving the health care provided ghetto residents. In addition, it was felt that such doctors would be better suited than their more conservatively oriented brethren to work cooperatively with local residents on programs aimed at bringing about greater community control of medical services. A decision was made to launch a search for some of these "socially conscious and politically aware" doctors to serve in Lincoln's pediatrics department.

The search involved not only officials at Lincoln, but also at the Albert Einstein College of Medicine. Under a contract with the city, Einstein College provides the medical and professional staffs for Lincoln and two other municipal hospitals in the Bronx. Dr. Arnold H. Einhorn, then director of pediatrics at Lincoln, recalls that the idea for the recruitment drive was first suggested to him by Dr. Lewis Fraad, chief of pediatrics at Einstein College. Fraad introduced Einhorn to four young residents who were interested in working on a program of community medicine.

The residents persuaded Einhorn that they could recruit the necessary interns. "My reaction at the time was, 'wonderful!'" Einhorn says. "Finally, I thought, white middle-class youths wanted to do something about poverty instead of just talking about it." The four residents prepared a recruiting brochure that was mailed to medical schools. As a result, the program managed to recruit thirty-two young interns, residents, and attending junior physicians for Lincoln's pediatrics department. Before taking up their positions, the thirty-two doctors met without Dr. Einhorn's knowledge and organized a group they called the Pediatrics Collective. They established two political priorities: First, a commitment to the idea that doctors should be fully responsible to the people they serve and that the community's views on hospital procedures should be solicited. Second, that an effort should be made to break down the traditional hierarchy that stratified and separated senior and junior medical personnel, nurses, and other hospital workers. Both of these priorities would later cause friction and turmoil at Lincoln Hospital.

Dr. Einhorn, who learned of the formation of the collective accidentally, says that one of its proposals called for Lincoln staff members to join in the operations of a health project sponsored by the Black Panthers. "I told them [collective members] we could not cooperate with racist groups," he says. Einhorn began to view the collective and the Lincoln recruitment program with misgivings. "I could see the handwriting on the wall," he says. These misgivings were heightened when the collective threw its weight behind reform proposals such as those made by the Young Lords. Among the most controversial proposals supported by the collective was one calling for "the total self-determination of all health services through a community-worker board" that would operate the hospital. Under the plan, community representatives would have had majority control of the proposed board—with final authority on such matters as hiring, firing, and budget priorities.

Numerous disputes arose between Einhorn and the collective—particularly over such groups as the Young Lords and the Black Panthers, with which the collective was willing to work. Gradually, the collective grew until it had forty-five active members and additional supporters on the hospital staff. At that point, the collective presented Einhorn with several position papers spelling out proposed reforms. He rejected the proposals. Twelve Korean and Filipino residents on Einhorn's pediatrics staff—who were not members of the collective—quit because of what they claimed was harassment by local residents accusing them of lacking commitment to ghetto medicine.

As if the situation were not serious enough, a new crisis arose—one that transcended the pediatrics department and involved the entire hospital. It was touched off when a nineteen-year-old woman named Carmen Rodriguez, who had been a participant in Lincoln's drug-rehabilitation program, died at the hospital after an abortion. A member of the collective named Dr. Michael Smith, who was a psychiatry resident, was called in to see her as she lay dying. He later

[101]

sharply criticized the hospital's handling of her case in an article published in a periodical circulated among residents and interns at all city hospitals.

"I decided not to go through channels," Smith wrote. "For once, there would be a complaint that is heard by all parties responsible. At that time, Lincoln had a patient complaint table staffed by activists from the South Bronx community. Together with representatives from the table, I went into the administrator's office and reported what I had read in the [patient's medical] chart." Smith contended the chart revealed mishandling of the case by the hospital staff.

His complaint led to demands by community groups for the ouster of Dr. Joseph J. Smith (no relation to Michael), Lincoln's director of obstetrics. Pamphlets distributed at the hospital by the community groups branded Dr. Joseph Smith as a "murderer." For a month, Dr. Smith was subjected to torrents of abuse from local residents. Finally, several of the more militant activists led him from the hospital grounds one day and warned him never to return. He was immediately transferred, at his own request, to the staff of another city hospital. The following day, all twenty-seven members of Lincoln's obstetrical staff walked off their jobs to protest the incident. They did not return for ten days.

Meanwhile, the rift in the hospital staff widened as a number of senior physicians demanded that criminal action be taken against the young psychiatrist, Dr. Michael Smith, for revealing confidential records about the death of Carmen Rodriguez. Dr. Elmer Foster, chief of radiology at Lincoln and president of the hospital's medical board, asked officials at Einstein College to press for such action. Foster says he was told by Dr. Labe Scheinberg, the college's dean, that the question should be handled through medical, rather than legal, channels. Scheinberg said the college would launch its own investigation. Later, however, an official of the college said that this investigation found "so much confusion . . . that it was impossible to know how the records became public."

In the months that followed, most participants and observers agree, *de facto* control of the hospital passed into the hands of the collective. Ultimately, Dr. Einhorn was transferred to another city hospital and replaced by a pediatrician from Puerto Rico, Dr. Helen Rodriguez. An investigation of the shift by the City Commission on Human Rights—responding to charges that Einhorn had been replaced because he was Jewish—resulted in a finding that no ethnic discrimination was involved. The commission called on all the diverse factions at Lincoln and in the surrounding community to seek means of reconciling their differences in the interest of improving health conditions. But there have been few indications to date of any such compromise. Periodic eruptions of discord continue to occur. For example, the staff of the psychiatric department has voted no confidence in its director for his refusal to sound out the community on a new drug program. About two dozen doctors at Lincoln have refused to bill patients for medical service in protest of anticipated budget cuts for municipal hospitals. And the heads of several departments at the hospital have said they intend to resign.

New York City's chief health official, Dr. Joseph English, says he is alarmed by the prospect of staff defections but "encouraged by the fact that new talent is being attracted to the hospital—talent that may be better equipped to handle the problems of the seventies than some of the older doctors, who may have battle fatigue." While welcoming the new talent, he expresses the hope that youthful enthusiasm for innovation will be tempered with an appreciation that traditional medical procedures do have some virtues. "We have some very idealistic young people who have to remember they are in training," English says. "I don't think they know the kind of dynamite they are playing with in the community.

I am sure that some of them are very well-trained physicians and socially responsible, but I've got a hunch that some of them are on the brink of irresponsibility."

While all of this may seem to the casual observer to represent a mere parochial dispute within the medical profession, its significance is far broader than that. The troubles at Lincoln Hospital are symptomatic of much of what is wrong in Hunts Point. The lack of adequate health care for Hunts Pointers and others in the Lincoln Hospital area is representative of the lack of numerous other essential city services. The reluctance of some officials to give local residents a voice in determining how municipal facilities shall be operated is representative of the paternalistic "we-know-what's-best-for-you" attitude assumed by many other public officials in dealing with denizens of Hunts Point and other ghettos. And the frustration and bitterness exhibited by the citizenry in demanding "a piece of the action" at Lincoln are representative of the emotions felt by Hunts Pointers on countless other issues.

What is most unusual about the Lincoln dispute is that, for once, the ghetto community has been able to mount a cooperative campaign to improve conditions in the area. True, this campaign created turmoil. True, it required leadership by groups such as the Young Lords and the Black Panthers —regarded by many in Hunts Point as irresponsible and extremist. True, tangible results of the campaign have not been far-ranging thus far. But some Hunts Pointers see the Lincoln affair as a hopeful sign—an indication that local residents will find ways to band together in the days ahead to fight for improved city services. The future of Hunts Point may well hang on the outcome of that prediction.

In the absence of concerted community action, however, many local residents feel that Hunts Pointers are doomed to permanent second-class citizenship. As an indication of the sort of treatment they receive from the city, they point to a recent event in Hunts Point. The City Department of Cultural Affairs, in cooperation with the Metropolitan Museum of Art, decided to try to give Hunts Point youngsters a bit of "cultural" experience. They sent a mobile art exhibit, mounted on a flatbed truck, into the neighborhood. For two weeks, the exhibit was on display at a site on Kelly Street— drawing flocks of interested children. There was no question about the good intentions of the city agency or the museum. But many Hunts Pointers, far from being grateful for the visiting exhibit, resented it. To them, it represented the worst sort of tokenism—the throwing of a crumb to a starving community.

"Man, with all we need in this area, that was like kicking us right in the ass," says one resident, Julio Maldonado. "We got people dying here because they don't have anything to eat. We got people dying because they live in filth or can't get a doctor to come to see them or don't have any heat in the wintertime. The money that was spent on that museum exhibit could have saved some lives if it was spent on something else. Sure, it was nice that the kids could see something like that. But for the city to send that in here for two weeks and then take it away—shit, man. . . . Is that supposed to satisfy us? Is that supposed to make up for everything else? We may not be very well educated around here, but we're not stupid. The city can't buy us off with that kind of bullshit!"

9

Anthony Zecca has had a series of near-perfect vantage points from which to witness Hunts Point's transformation from garden spot to ghetto. First, as a child, he played in the green fields and farms that dotted the neighborhood almost four decades ago. He then went to school in Hunts Point. Next, while operating a small grocery and meat market, he watched the area "begin going to hell" during the early 1950's. And, since 1956, he has seen with angry, saddened eyes the worst horrors Hunts Point has to offer; he has been assigned to his old neighborhood all that time as a policeman.

It would be hard to find anyone who knows Hunts Point better than Tony Zecca. From the top of his head, he can rattle off names and addresses of countless residents—past and present. He knows who used to operate what store at which address; what's there now; what's happened to the old-timers. He knows the hangouts of the current-day junkies, thieves, pimps, and whores. His attitude about Hunts Point can best be described as a love-hate relationship: he loves what it used to be and hates what it has become.

"Ah, what can I say about the people here now?" he asks. "Some of them are OK, but a lot of them are nothing but wild Indians." The word "Indian," in referring to Hunts Pointers, is used frequently around the 41st Precinct station house on Simpson Street—from which Tony operates as a patrolman. The precinct house, in fact, is nicknamed "Fort Apache." The name dates back to an incident about a half-dozen years ago. Tony, making an appearance in court, was greeted by a policeman from another precinct. "How are things in Fort Apache?" the other officer asked.

"Fort Apache? What do you mean?"

"That's what I call your [precinct] house. It seems like it's always under attack by the Indians."

When Tony returned to the station house, he related the story to other officers, and the name stuck. Today, in their off-duty hours, men from the 41st wear sweatshirts and T-shirts emblazoned: FORT APACHE.

"It's hard to believe what Hunts Point is like today if you know what it used to be like," Tony says. "When I was a kid, it was the greatest place in the world to grow up."

Tony was brought to Hunts Point at the age of three. He had been born on December 26, 1931, in a house on St. Lawrence Avenue—several miles north of Hunts Point. His father, Antonio, had emigrated to the United States from the island of Ponza, Italy, at the age of six. As a young boy, Antonio Zecca had worked as a water-hauler in a lumber camp in West Virginia where his father had been employed. Later, he had moved to the Bronx and become, successively, a marble-setter, a shipyard worker, and a building contractor. Tony's mother, named Sophie, was American-born. She, her husband, and Tony moved in 1935 from the house on St. Lawrence Avenue into a small walkup apartment building at 795 Barry Street in Hunts Point.

"We lived in Apartment 14; it was just three rooms, but eventually five of us lived there very comfortably," Tony says. (His mother later gave birth to a daughter, Rosalie, three years Tony's junior, and another son, Silverio, five years his junior.) "That apartment building was immaculate," Tony recalls. "You'd never see a cigarette butt or a loose piece of paper around the lobby or hallways. There were beautiful curtains on the windows in the lobby and a rug on the lobby floor. Nobody in the house ever locked a door. Everybody knew everybody else and visited back and forth."

Across the street from the apartment house was a vacant lot. "One of the men in the building, named Jack Storcey, started farming on the land in the lot," Tony says. "Storcey didn't own the land or rent it, but the owner didn't care. He was glad to have somebody looking after the place. Before long, Storcey had everything under the sun growing there—corn, tomatoes, you name it. He kept chickens and goats there, too. Every now and then, the goats would get loose and go running all over the neighborhood."

The section of Hunts Point in which Tony and his family lived was known as the Springhurst area. In those days, about ninety-five percent of its residents were Italian-Americans. The others were mainly of Irish, Jewish, or Polish stock. "It's almost all occupied now by Puerto Ricans or blacks, but a few of the Italian families are still there," Tony says. "On Longwood Avenue, between Barry and Tiffany Streets, there used to be seven beautiful private houses. Only two of them are still left; the others were ruined—looted, vandalized, and burned out—and finally torn down. But the two that are still there are occupied by old Italian families that have been there for years, the D'Amores and the Cardillos. One of the D'Amores, Eugene, was a good friend of mine. In fact, he was an usher at my wedding."

During Tony's youth, life in his neighborhood was governed by a variety of rituals. "Take Sundays, for instance," he says. "Everything that happened there on Sundays was a ritual. We'd all get up early on Sundays and go to Mass at St. Athanasius Church. If you were a teen-aged boy and you had a steady girlfriend, it was a big thing to walk with her to church. That let everybody know the two of you were going together and the two families approved. It was like an Easter Parade every Sunday—everybody all dressed up and promenading to and from the church. In our building, just about everybody was Catholic—so the whole building would empty out on Sunday mornings. Even then, nobody would lock the apartment doors. If some thieves had wanted to, they could have come in there and cleaned out every apartment in the place. But we didn't have that kind of problem in those days; we didn't even concern ourselves about it. You just went out and left the door unlocked. And, when you came back, nothing had been touched."

After church, there was another ritual—the weekly neighborhood stickball game. "We played on Longwood Avenue, between Garrison Avenue and Barry Street," Tony recalls. "All the young married men and the teen-aged boys would get in the game. And the whole neighborhood came out and watched. There was always a lot of friendly betting. Then, on Sunday afternoons, there was still another ritual. Everybody would gather in the back yard of a family named Foglio that lived in a small private house on Barry Street, near Worthen Street, next to a pickle works. The Foglios made wine in their basement. They'd serve wine to everybody on Sundays. Somebody else usually brought some food. It was like a little festival every Sunday afternoon. There was a *boccie* court in the yard, and all the older men would play. [*Boccie* is an Italian lawn-bowling game.] The Foglios were an interesting family. They had a pet crow named Cheche. One time, Cheche got loose and we didn't know whether he'd ever come back. It was like a neighborhood disaster. Everybody in the neighborhood went out looking for him. Finally, somebody retrieved him, and there was an extra celebration that week in the Foglios' yard."

Nearby, on a site along the East River near what is now the intersection of Ryawa Avenue and Barretto Street but in those days consisted of a couple of unmarked dirt roads, there was an open field dotted with cherry trees. Local residents called it Cherry Point Park. And on Sunday afternoons the neighborhood's Polish-American families gathered there for festivals of their own. In warm weather, they would swim in the river.

Also nearby was a dairy called Gold Medal Farms, which distributed milk products throughout the area. "I used to go down there every other day when I was a kid to see if I could pick up a piece of free ice to put in the old icebox we had in our apartment," Tony recalls. "Usually, somebody there would let me have a spare piece. But, if there was none around, I'd go to an ice plant on Worthen Street and buy a big chunk for fifteen cents, put it on my shoulder, and haul it home. We didn't have much money in those days, so fifteen cents was a big investment that we tried to save whenever we could."

At another spot along the East River, where there is now a city dock, near Tiffany Street, the marshy fields were filled with ducks, pheasants, and other wild game during Tony's youth. "They're all gone now," he says. "There used to be an inlet there and the water used to come inland about three blocks farther than it does now. The area was filled in and paved streets were put in—back to what's now East Bay Avenue. Old-timers have told me that, back during Prohibition, Dutch Schultz used to bring some of his boats in there with smuggled liquor. The booze was unloaded into trucks and taken to a warehouse around Whitlock Avenue. It was beautiful down there when I was a kid—all those pheasants and ducks and all. Now, it's just like the rest of Hunts Point —a mess. Ah, I hate to even think about it."

From kindergarten through eighth grade, Tony attended P.S. 48. At the age of nine, he began working after school at the B&B Restaurant on Barry Street at Longwood Avenue. "I swept the floor, filled the egg crates, unpacked the supplies

—just generally helped around the place. The restaurant was owned by a man named Hammer. One of Mr. Hammer's brothers owned a stable down around Barretto Street; there were still horses in Hunts Point in the forties. At the restaurant, I got paid two dollars a week at first, then was raised to three. Believe it or not, with that money, I saved enough to buy my father a three-hundred-dollar car—a 1937 Plymouth. This must have been about 1943 or so. Mr. Hammer eventually sold the restaurant to a man named Herman Goslinski, who kept me on. The restaurant's still there and still owned by the Goslinski family. Herman's son, Sol, is running it."

After graduation from P.S. 48, Tony entered Stuyvesant High School—the school for gifted students in Lower Manhattan. Although attendance there required an hour-long subway ride in each direction, Tony still found time for an after-school job. He gave up the restaurant job and went to work as a twelve-dollar-a-week delivery boy at a small grocery and butcher shop on Longwood Avenue owned by a man named Adolph Geis. About 1946, Geis sold the shop to a kindly but businesslike man named Otto Staats. "Mr. Staats was wonderful to me," Tony recalls. "He treated me like a son, promoted me from delivery boy to his general assistant around the store, and really taught me the business. He taught me how to cut meat—everything. He also raised my salary to eighteen dollars a week."

Meanwhile, Tony had acquired a steady girlfriend. Her name was Anne Marie Zurzolo, and she lived right across the hall from him in Apartment 12 at 795 Barry Street. At the age of thirteen, Anne had moved into the building with her family from a private house nearby on Burnet Place. "That Burnet Place, even in the forties, was like a street out in a little country town," Tony says. "There were about eight beautiful one-family houses—all with beautiful trees and yards. Then, a short distance away, it was very citified. There was a baking factory called Your Baking Company. We used to go in there and buy a big bag of fresh buns for a dime."

Once Tony and Anne started going steady, they followed the familiar pattern of walking to church together. Their dates consisted mostly of going to one of the four movie houses in Hunts Point—the Loew's Spooner, the Loew's Boulevard, the Art, and the Star. The Star, on Southern Boulevard near 163rd Street, was a Saturday favorite of Hunts Point youngsters. For a quarter, they could spend practically the entire day there—watching three full-length action pictures, a couple of Western serials, cartoons, a newsreel, and previews of coming attractions. Sometimes there was even a game of Screeno—a Bingolike affair in which prizes were awarded. Hardly a kid who entered the Star on Saturday came without a paper bag containing his lunch and, in some cases, even his dinner. Today, the Star, the Art, and the Boulevard are still in business, chiefly showing Spanish-language films. The Spooner has been converted into a furniture store.

By 1949, although Tony and Anne were only seventeen, they were seriously contemplating marriage. Tony was in his senior year at Stuyvesant High, and was still working at Otto Staats' shop. By that time, the influx of Negroes and Puerto Ricans had begun and Hunts Point had started to deteriorate. The situation was far from critical yet, but danger signs had appeared. No longer could apartment doors be left unlocked; the neighborhood was beginning to experience a noticeable increase in crime.

"One Sunday, Mr. Staats went down to the store just to check on things," Tony recalls. "The store was closed on Sundays, but either he or I usually stopped by to see if everything was all right and to feed the cats we kept there. When Mr. Staats opened the door, he found three or four guys inside. They'd broken in through the back of the store. When they saw him, they ran out and he chased after them. While he was running, Mr. Staats had a stroke; he died a little while later."

Staats' widow was unable to carry on the business and said she planned to sell it. Tony, who felt he knew enough about the business to run it on his own, decided to try to take it over. "I still had six months to go in high school, but all I was interested in at the time was getting married and making money," Tony says. "I decided that, if I could buy the store from Mrs. Staats, I'd quit school and run the store full-time. I went to my father and told him what I wanted to do. He'd been doing some contracting—building houses up at Valhalla, New York. He had about five thousand saved up—his life's savings. I told him the store would be a great investment; Mr. Staats had been making money with it and I was sure I could, too. My father agreed to put up the money and Mrs. Staats agreed to let us have the store for the five thousand. So I quit school and took over the store. My mother helped me run it. My father continued in the contracting business. I was right about the store being a money-maker. In no time, I made back the five thousand we'd invested."

On June 4, 1950, Tony and Anne—both eighteen years old—were married in St. Athanasius Church. They lived briefly with his parents, then bought a house at 1443 Merry Avenue in the Pelham Bay section of the Bronx. His parents continued living in the apartment house on Barry Street. The grocery-butcher shop continued to prosper for a time. But, as the neighborhood deteriorated, so did the business. The steady influx of Negroes and Puerto Ricans, the rising crime rate, and the general atmosphere of despair that settled over Hunts Point all contrived to drive away the people who had been Tony's best customers. In the building where he had grown up, for example, old-time tenants were leaving in droves. Tony's parents remained, but most of their long-time neighbors were gone by the middle of the 1950's. The new residents who took their places, strapped for money, tended to do their shopping in cut-rate supermarkets rather than small shops such as Tony's.

Tony sensed that, although he might be able to make a living out of the business for several years more, there was no long-range future there for a man of his age. Thus, he decided to become a policeman. His father gave up his contracting enterprise to work full-time at the store with Tony's mother. By that time, although Tony had never finished his remaining six months of high school, he had passed a test qualifying him for a high-school-equivalency diploma. He entered the New York City Police Academy on June 13, 1956, and after graduation was assigned, by coincidence, to the 41st Precinct—patrolling the very streets where he'd grown up. He has been there ever since.

He has seen those streets he used to love taken over by the "Indians," as he calls them. He has had bullets fired at him on those streets, been thrown down a flight of stairs in an apartment house that once was among the finest in the neighborhood. "It makes me sick what's happened to Hunts Point," he says.

"Take the building where I grew up. It kept getting worse and worse, but my parents didn't want to move. Then, one day in 1965, they came home and found the door broken open. Everything they owned—I mean everything—had been stolen. Now, you know somebody can't just empty out a whole apartment without being seen. But there hadn't been a single complaint to the police. As far as we know, nobody had tried to stop these Indians from hauling the whole place away. That was it, as far as I was concerned. My brother-in-law and I made my parents move that very day into my brother-in-law's house on Staten Island."

His parents closed down their store and began trying to sell it, but could find no takers. They eventually unloaded it for a mere thousand dollars. Meanwhile, the apartment house on Barry Street, where they had lived for thirty years, continued to lose its long-time tenants. "There's only one of them left today—Mary Storcey, the wife of the guy who'd planted the farm in the vacant lot across the street," Tony says.

"And she's had a helluva rough time there. She's come to me any number of times since I've been on the police force to report she's been robbed by junkies. We've never been able to catch any of them. She's scared to death living there, but she just hasn't moved for some reason. You should see the building now. People just urinate and defecate in the hallways and on the staircases. The windows are broken; the place is falling apart. I've been inside the apartment where we used to live. The ceiling is coming down. The walls have big holes in them and obscenities written all over them. The windows are broken. I tell you, it's unbelievable. The people who live in that building now just don't care about anything; they're animals."

The lot across the street that once bloomed with Jack Storcey's crops was eventually used as the site for a Gulf Oil service station. "But even that was destroyed," Tony says. "Thieves and vandals tore it apart." All that remains now is the shell of the building—resembling the ruins in a bombed city.

"At 1202 Spofford Avenue, there's an elevator apartment house that used to be quite the place to live in Hunts Point," Tony says. "It was a beautiful building—immaculate, with handsome furniture in the lobby. Today, you take your life in your hands going into the place. There've been a couple of homicides in the building. In one, I remember, someone fired a rifle through an apartment door and killed an occupant of the apartment. One time, when I was making an arrest there, I got thrown down a flight of stairs before I could finally make the pinch.

"Another time, Thanksgiving Day of 1968, I was called to

meet a complainant who said a shot had been fired at him from a house at 627 Manida Street. Years ago, Manida Street was beautiful, too—all those private houses with trees out front and big back yards. There never used to be any trouble there. Now, it's a jungle, too. Lots of times, when we get calls in this neighborhood from people claiming they've had shots fired at them, we're skeptical. Many times, we go out and find it's a false alarm. But, when my partner and I got to this house on Manida Street, the complainant was waiting on the street and really seemed scared. He yelled to us: 'You better watch out! There's a guy in the house with a rifle!' Just then, the guy inside opened the front door of the house and fired a shot at me. It didn't miss by much. My partner and I pulled out our service revolvers and rushed up beside the house. My partner picked up a garbage can and heaved it through a window of the house to distract the guy with the rifle. Then I broke down the front door and we rushed in. We were lucky—and so was he. We were able to subdue him without any more shots being fired. I don't know what that guy's problem was; maybe he was psycho. I never found out why he'd started shooting."

As a policeman, Tony has encountered every type of crime that plagues Hunts Point—murder, assault, armed robbery, burglary, grand and petty larceny, narcotics possession and sale, prostitution, and the rest. "It keeps getting worse all the time," he says. "Right now, it's getting more serious than ever—particularly down at the Hunts Point Market. The market's become a haven for prostitutes. After these truck drivers come in from a long haul, many of them are looking for some female companionship, so it's natural that prostitutes would try to hang out there. With them come the pimps, the junk dealers, and the thieves. There's a lot of merchandise lying around there, just waiting to be stolen. So the market's really become a plum to be picked by any criminal who's looking for a score."

So pervasive have the crime problems become in Hunts Point, Tony says, that many merchants buy safes they don't even bother to lock. "They just use the safes for fire protection for their valuables," he says. "They don't lock them, because they'd rather just let the thieves have what's inside than take the chance that the thieves will break the safes open with sledgehammers. This way, at least they don't have to buy a new safe every time they're burglarized. They can keep on using the same unlocked safe for fire protection."

Equally disturbing to Tony as these crimes for profit are the senseless, profitless acts of vandalism that are making the neighborhood ever more ugly and depressing. "After World War II, the city created a little park in a triangular plot of ground where Spofford Avenue meets Tiffany Street and Longwood Avenue," he says. "It was named Corporal Walter Fufidio Park, for a fellow from the neighborhood who was killed in the battle of Iwo Jima. A small monument was put there and a flagpole and some benches. Back when I was a kid, the American flag used to be flown there every day. The place was a sort of quiet refuge; everybody respected it because it was dedicated to the memory of one of our local heroes. People would even pick up pieces of paper that blew in there. Now you should see it. Vandals have broken the monument and torn up all the benches. Nobody bothers to fly the flag there any more. The kids hang onto the rope that used to be used to raise the flag and just swing around the flagpole on it. The park looks like a disaster area."

Tony was involved in the campaign to repair the damage done by vandals to the cemetery where poet Joseph Rodman Drake is buried. "After the cemetery was torn up, a bunch of people pitched in to fix it up," he says. "My brother-in-law, William Lassourreille, and I helped out. My brother-in-law works as a stone-cutter for a company in Hunts Point, Metropolitan Stone Products at Lafayette Avenue and Drake

Street. He made a granite monument, had it engraved with some appropriate words, and contributed it for the ceremonies when the cemetery was rededicated after the vandalism damage was repaired. The kids from P.S. 48 came down for the ceremonies and planted a tree near where the monument was placed. The ceremonies were very nice. But a short time later, the cemetery was desecrated again. The monument and the new tree were both damaged. They're still there, but nobody takes care of the cemetery any more. The Parks Department, which has jurisdiction over the cemetery, finally threw up its hands and gave up."

Tony now lives in Dongan Hills, Staten Island, with his wife and their three children—Linda, who is twenty, and sixteen-year-old twins, Joseph and Anthony, Jr. But, as much as he hates what Hunts Point has become, a section of his heart of hearts retains its old love for the place. He hopes, knowing it is the longest of long shots, that something can be done to restore Hunts Point to some facsimile of the idyllic spot he remembers from his youth. But what, he was asked, can be done?

"The main thing is to educate the people here now that *they're* the ones who live here," he replies. "If they tear the buildings apart, it's *their* buildings—the places where *they* live. If they toss broken bottles in the streets, it's *their* car tires that are going to get flats. If they urinate and defecate in the hallways of the buildings, *they're* the ones who're going to smell it and step in it. We're not talking about the color of people's skins; we're talking about what's inside their minds. The people have to develop a sense of pride. They have to want to do something to help themselves."

The next chapter will describe how some Hunts Pointers, who had sunk to the depths of depravity and despair, *are* trying to do something to help themselves.

10

Lena T. is seventeen years old. She has a delicate Latin face, wide brown eyes, a slim waist, a firm bosom, and long, slender legs. For three of her seventeen years, she has sold her body as a prostitute in Hunts Point.

Alberto R. is twenty years old. He has a flat, rugged face, brown eyes, short legs, and a wiry build. For five of his twenty years, he has been a thief in Hunts Point.

There are several common denominators between Lena and Alberto. Both came to New York as children from Puerto Rico—Lena from Ponce and Alberto from San Juan. Both had families living on welfare payments. Both were school dropouts. Both moved to Hunts Point because their families could find no less expensive place to live. But the greatest common denominator between them is that both have had their lives deeply scarred by heroin addiction and both are making genuine attempts to kick the habit and lead productive, fruitful lives.

"Everything went wrong for me in such a hurry that I can't believe it even now," Lena says. "When I was a kid, I always did what my parents told me—I was a good kid, you know. We were poor, on welfare because my father couldn't find a job. But I didn't think too much about it. It wasn't unusual in this neighborhood. A lot of our neighbors were on welfare, too. We had seven mouths to feed—my mother, my father, me and my three sisters, and my brother. I'm the oldest kid, so I tried to find a job, but nobody'd hire me, either."

When she was thirteen and in the eighth grade, Lena says, she acquired her first boyfriend. His name was Manuel, but everybody called him Manny. He was fifteen. "Up till then, I felt like a nobody," Lena recalls. "But Manny was one of the real 'wheels' in the neighborhood. Being his girlfriend made me feel important. I'd have done anything he wanted." She did just about everything Manny wanted—losing her virginity to him in an apartment-house basement when she was not quite thirteen and a half.

"I'd like to be able to blame him, but he really didn't have to persuade me a lot," she says. "I wanted to do it. The first time, it hurt a little but I liked it anyway. After the first time, I really loved it. I don't know, maybe I'm oversexed or something. But I'm not ashamed to say it: I really love to screw."

It was Manny who introduced Lena to drugs. He was using heroin when she met him, but made no effort at first to lure her onto hard drugs. "After we'd been going together for about a month, he offered me some *pitos* [marijuana cigarettes]," she recalls. "I tried one and, to tell you the truth, it didn't do much to me. I'd smoked regular cigarettes before, and this didn't seem much different. I smoked a few more *pitos* and I began to feel real good; it seemed like everything was *so* beautiful. Manny took me down to that basement again and made love to me and I thought it was the greatest. I figured if the *pitos* could make sex that good, I'd smoke them all the time."

It was a short step from marijuana to heroin. Manny convinced her, she says, that heroin would make sex and everything else in her life seem even more beautiful than marijuana had. So she let him give her a light "fix." He did not inject it into a "mainline" (vein), but merely gave her a "skin-popping" (a needle prick that lightly penetrated the skin of her arm). "It was like with the first time I tried *pitos*," Lena says. "It didn't give me much of a jolt. So Manny gave me a few more skin-pops and I began to feel it. Man, I tell you, it felt cool. I knew where I was and all, but it was like nothing bad could ever happen to me. I felt so fuckin' good. They say heroin takes away from your interest in sex, but it wasn't that way with me. Manny laid me again, and it was even better than before."

Gradually, Lena moved from occasional skin-popping to regular skin-popping to occasional mainlining and finally became a full-fledged heroin addict. By the time she was fourteen, she had a fifty-dollar-a-day habit. Manny had dropped her for another girl, but she had another boyfriend named Eduardo and called Eddie. Also an addict, Eddie was nineteen and had been stealing from stores and apartments to support his habit. At first, he helped support Lena's habit as well—but in time he insisted she start paying her own way.

"He told me he wanted to turn me out," Lena says, using a term that means Eddie wanted to turn her into a prostitute and become her pimp. "Eddie knew a bunch of the pimps in the neighborhood and he knew how they operated. He figured he could make more money turning me out than he could stealing, so he asked me if I'd do it. Well, you know, I was just a kid—fourteen—but I looked about eighteen or nineteen. I was very well developed. I'd never thought about becoming a prostitute, but when Eddie asked me I didn't get upset or nothing like that. I didn't think I had no choice. Eddie said he wouldn't get me no more junk unless I went on the street for him. I needed the stuff bad, I couldn't do without it. A couple of times, when Eddie couldn't get no junk because there was a panic and our suppliers didn't have none, I thought I'd die. I had these real bad cramps and chills and then sweating spells. Man, it was the worst. So I told Eddie I'd do it. I dropped out of school and started hustling full-time."

Lena says she and Eddie hung around the corner of Simpson Street and Westchester Avenue, the prostitution hub of Hunts Point, looking for customers. Within a couple of hours, Eddie had lined up Lena's first "John"—a Puerto Rican man about forty. "I was nervous, but in a way I was sort of looking forward to it," Lena recalls. "Like I said, I enjoy sex a whole lot. It didn't matter to me that this was a guy I'd never seen before. To me, it was a chance to have some fun in bed and get paid for it, too. Anyway, Eddie just asked the guy for six bucks. Most of the girls hustling around there were making at least eight a trick, but Eddie just asked for six because he was anxious to get me started. Eddie took us to a little beat-up hotel a short distance away. He rented a room there for the day. I took the guy inside and asked him if there was anything special he wanted me to do. He wasn't too particular. He just told me to take off my clothes and lie on the bed. So I did. He got on top of me and, in a couple of minutes, it was all over. It was a big disappointment to me. I mean, I was used to having men try to do something for me, too, in bed. But this guy just took care of himself, then climbed off and started getting dressed. Well, I figured, at least we had his money, and maybe the next John would be better."

Some of the succeeding Johns were better, but most were about as unexciting for Lena as the first. Nonetheless, she did not think prostitution was a bad life at first. "Maybe it wasn't all a lot of sexual kicks, but I got some pleasure out of it once in a while," she says. "Besides, I was making the bread Eddie and I needed to buy junk. And, when I got finished working for the day, I could always get some good sex from Eddie."

But, just as she had been jilted by Manny, she was eventually ditched by Eddie as well. He found another girl, turned her out as a prostitute, and dropped Lena. Actually, Eddie had wanted to have both girls working for him—and Lena was willing—but the new girl insisted on being Eddie's one and only. There followed a steady stream of pimps in Lena's life. All except the last one treated her "fairly well," as she puts it. But the last, named Tony, treated her brutally.

"Tony was a mean son of a bitch," she says. "He just liked to hurt people. He used to beat the hell out of me for no reason. I did my best to make a lot of bread for him, but he was never satisfied. I'd come back from turning a trick and, without saying a word, he'd just start beating me up."

By that time Lena was seventeen, had been a prostitute for three years, and had a "burning" heroin habit that was costing her fifty dollars a day. Since Tony's habit was almost as severe as her own, she had to turn at least ten tricks a day—even though her price had risen from the original six to ten and an occasional twelve. She had long since moved from her parents' apartment and was living with Tony. Without him, she would have neither a roof over her head nor a source of heroin. But her life had become such a series of torments that she decided she had to do something drastic to change it.

"Tony had me filling dates with all kinds of weirdos—especially guys like him who liked to beat girls up," she says. "With them beating the shit out of me, and Tony, too, I couldn't take it any more. I decided the only way I could straighten up was to quit being a prostitute, kick the H habit, and get away from Tony. The toughest part would be kicking the habit."

How Lena went about trying to do so will be described later in this chapter. Her experiences in attempting to give up heroin closely paralleled those of Alberto R., the twenty-year-old thief.

Alberto had come to Hunts Point when he was eleven. He lived with his parents, an older brother, and two younger sisters. His father was able to find work only sporadically, so the family was forced to rely on welfare payments. Until he was thirteen, Alberto was considered a "good boy." He went to school regularly, was a plugger if not a scholar, minded his parents, went to church, and kept his nose clean. At thirteen, however, he fell in with a group of older boys regarded as the "tough guys" of their immediate neighborhood. Because he wanted to be "one of the gang," Alberto says, he went along with the various escapades of the others. At first, these involved petty acts of vandalism—breaking a window or turning over a crate of apples standing outside a produce store. Gradually, the offenses became more serious—extorting small amounts of money from other teen-agers with the threat of beatings; smoking and selling marijuana; then moving on to using pills and, finally, heroin.

"I started mainlining when I was fifteen," Alberto says. "From then on, I had to steal to support my habit. "Mostly, I'd break into apartments when nobody was home. There usually was no cash in the places, so I'd take a television set or a stereo or a piece of small furniture if it looked like it was worth anything. Some of the older guys I hung out with knew a fence who'd buy anything if it had any value at all. So I started dealing with this fence, and he'd give me about half of what the stuff was worth. At first, my habit was just costing me about twenty bucks a day. So, if I stole a TV or a stereo worth a couple of hundred bucks, the fence would maybe let me have a hundred, and that would buy my junk for the next five days or so."

During the next five years, however, Alberto ran his habit up to about fifty dollars a day. Thus, he was forced to steal merchandise worth at least twice that amount every day in order to get enough money from the fence to provide the heroin his body craved. "Man, I was living just for the needle," he says. "I was running around like a madman, stealing all the time. Sometimes, when I'd have a run of bad luck and couldn't steal anything valuable, I'd go out of my fuckin' mind until I could make a score and get some more junk."

Alberto was arrested three times during the five years. The first time, the police couldn't make a case on him and he was released. The second time, he was given juvenile-offender treatment by the courts and freed on probation. The third time, he was convicted of burglary and sentenced to six months in jail, but released after three months. "The time I was in the can didn't do a thing for me," he says. "Nobody tried to give me any training so I could get a job when I got out. Nobody did anything to keep me from going right back to junk as soon as I hit the street."

Thus, within a day after his release, he had pulled another burglary and immediately bought some heroin. "I was back on the same old merry-go-round," he says. "Steal something, fence it, buy some junk, shoot up, then go looking for something else to steal." He had dropped out of school at sixteen and had never done an honest day's work. Although he continued living with his family, his relations with his parents were so strained that he often didn't talk to them for weeks at a time. "My old man kept threatening to toss me out on my ass if I didn't shape up, but he didn't have the balls to go through with it," Alberto says.

What eventually made him decide to try to turn his life around was the death of one of his addict friends. "His name was Arthur, but we called him Duke for some reason—I don't know why, but that's what everybody called him," Alberto says. "He used to hang out with the same bunch of guys I did. Once in a while, Duke and I would go together on a score and split whatever we got from the fence. We turned on together a lot. One day, he was off by himself and shot up. Some of the guys found him later in the basement of an abandoned building. He was deader than hell. He must have OD'd [overdosed], or maybe somebody gave him a bad load of junk. Anyway, he was dead. I'd heard a lot about people dying from junk, but this was the first time it happened to anyone I knew well. It hit me real hard. I started thinking, for the first time in a helluva long while, about what I was doing with my life. I had a picture of some of my buddies finding me someday just like Duke—deader than hell. Well, I decided I was gonna try to straighten up. I didn't make myself any promises; I didn't know if I had the balls to kick [the habit]. But I just made up my mind to take a shot at it and see what happened."

When Alberto R. and Lena T. decided to try to kick the heroin habit, both sought the help of drug-rehabilitation centers in Hunts Point. There are several such centers in the neighborhood, succeeding to various degrees in weaning addicts off heroin and other drugs. The best known is a pioneering operation known as SERA—Services in Education and Rehabilitation for Addiction. Headquartered in two formerly abandoned buildings at 1010 and 1014 Hoe Avenue, Sera is sponsored by an organization known as the Hispanic Association for a Drug-Free Society.

SERA is essentially the product of an idea formulated by a former addict named Frank Gracia. In 1967, Gracia, who had been hooked on heroin for twenty-two years, was serving time on a drug charge at Rikers Island—a prison situated on an island in the East River a short distance off Hunts Point. The prison, among other things, served as an induction center for Phoenix House, a voluntary drug-rehabilitation project operated by former addicts. Prisoners who wanted to enter the Phoenix House program were screened at Rikers Island before their release. Gracia became inmate-coordinator of the screening project. He discovered in his work that sixty-five percent of those involved in the induction program at Rikers Island were Spanish-speaking inmates. And of those, ninety percent were school dropouts—chiefly because of the language barrier. Most spoke only broken English; some spoke no English at all.

After his own release from Rikers Island and the curing of his drug habit, Gracia became project director of Phoenix House. He became convinced that, although Phoenix House did much constructive work with addicts, neither it nor any other drug-rehabilitation project in the country filled two basic needs—the offering of a bilingual program for Spanish-speaking addicts and of a program that would completely rehabilitate an addict within a year. Although many Spanish-speaking addicts were involved in rehabilitation programs, there was none designed specifically to cope with their needs. As a result, many of them dropped out of the programs and went back on drugs. Most rehabilitation programs lasted from eighteen months to three years. Gracia felt that was much too long—that the long duration minimized the chances of success.

Gracia and Frank Marrero, another former Rikers Island inmate who had worked in the Phoenix House project, discussed the need for a bilingual one-year program with a third man interested in drug-rehabilitation work, Sal Lucania. Together, they drew up a proposal for such a program and submitted it to the New York State Narcotics Addiction Control Commission. The commission agreed to make a $1.3 million grant to establish the program, which ultimately became known as SERA. Gracia became executive director of SERA, Marrero became his deputy, and Lucania became the program's chief administrator.

They persuaded the owner of the two abandoned tenements on Hoe Avenue to spend $400,000 to renovate the buildings for use as SERA's headquarters. SERA pays the owner $140,000 a year in rent for the buildings, which provide 40,000 square feet of floor space. The program went into operation in June, 1970.

On the ground floor of the building at 1014 Hoe Avenue is an attractive office occupied by Dennis Ferrigno, SERA's director of community development. It has paneled walls, handsome blue and white drapes, an imitation of an antique clock, a black leather couch, a conference table, a low cocktail table bearing an arrangement of dried flowers, several colorful paintings, a large desk, and a comfortable desk chair. At first glance, it seems a trifle incongruous when compared with the miserable slum conditions that can be viewed through Ferrigno's office window. But, when one considers that the purposes of the SERA center include helping the addicts who pass through this office to pull themselves up out of the slums, the attractiveness of the office seems a handy device for reminding them that there is another world out there besides the world of the ghetto.

Ferrigno is a handsome young man who wears mod clothes—complete with a medallion hanging from his neck —and can speak either the hip language of the streets or the jargon of the social worker. He alternates between the two as he explains how the SERA program works.

"What's different about our program—besides the fact that it's bilingual and that it rehabilitates an addict in just one year—is that we offer total services," Ferrigno says. "Those words, 'total services,' are very important. Most drug programs offer only rehabilitation. Our program has four components—rehabilitation, community development and organization, a youth component, and education."

The words sound impressive, but what do they mean? What is involved in each of these four components? What happens to an addict who comes to SERA for help?

"All right, let's say an addict has just come to us," Ferrigno says. "He might have come on his own or he might have been referred to us by some agency. He's not necessarily a Spanish-speaking person. Although the program is designed for Spanish-speaking people, we don't limit it to them. We'll take anyone." (Of the first 133 addicts enrolled in the program, 107 were Spanish-speaking, 23 were Negroes, and 3 were Caucasians.) "So this addict comes to us and says he wants to kick drugs. Typically, he—or she—is on heroin. We get some pill-heads and some grass-smokers, but mostly it's heroin.

"The first thing that happens is that we send the addict to our induction center, right nearby at 1081 East 165th Street —just off Hoe Avenue. He's detoxified, either by putting him in a hospital temporarily or by treating him on an out-patient basis. During the detoxification period, he's given methadone, a drug designed to ease addicts' withdrawal symptoms and block the high provided by heroin. Unlike many other programs, which provide former addicts with methadone on a continuing basis, we don't use methadone once the detoxification period is over. That usually takes four to six weeks. After that, the addict doesn't get any kind of drugs. During the detoxification period, he attends our induction program from nine o'clock in the morning until five in the afternoon, five days a week. We try to motivate him to really want to kick the habit. We use encounter sessions, private discussions —whatever we think will motivate him best. Once he passes through our screening process and satisfies us that he really wants to be rehabilitated, we send him on to what we call our therapeutic community.

"At that point, he's going to be living in, twenty-four hours a day, at our building at 1010 Hoe Avenue. Usually, he's going to need welfare payments if he has a family outside that needs support. So we take him down and get him signed up for welfare. We're very careful, in our screening process, to eliminate anyone we think is coming into the program simply to get on the welfare rolls.

"The therapeutic community is a residential live-in situation, all day, seven days a week. An addict usually stays there from three to six months. The therapeutic community is a duplication of the outside world. Each person has a work function. Maybe he works in the kitchen or cleans up the place as a porter, but he has something to do. Actually, we try to give each person a job that's completely different from what he wants to do, because that's the way things are in the outside world. When he leaves here, he's most likely going to have to take a job that he doesn't feel is suited to his talents or his desires. So we try to prepare him for that here—to teach him to accept responsibility. He attends three encounter sessions a week, five seminars, five meetings, and various rap sessions and tutorial groups.

"Everything a person gets in the therapeutic community must be earned. For example, if he wants to spend a weekend at home or have a visit from his wife or have a private room, he has to prove he deserves it by accepting every responsibility that's given to him. We hope that will give him a different point of view and help him know the value of what he's got."

There are both men and women living in the therapeutic community. They have separate sleeping quarters, but virtually all the activities are carried out on a co-ed basis. One of the most important activities is an educational program. "We have a principal and ten licensed teachers in our education department," Ferrigno says. "Attendance at our school is mandatory for two hours every day. Each class has only four or five students, so each person gets much more individualized attention than he would in a public school. All the teachers speak English and Spanish. We've had fantastic results with most of the students. Some of them couldn't speak, read, or write any English when they came here. Now they're able to do all three. We feel that ought to be a great help to them when they go back outside and go looking for jobs."

After his three to six months in the therapeutic community, the reformed addict moves on to what SERA calls the day-care part of its program. At first, he continues to spend twenty-four hours a day on the premises but is given additional privileges while his progress is being evaluated. If his progress has been satisfactory, he is then eligible to take an outside job while continuing to spend his off-duty hours at the SERA center. Finally, he both works and lives on the outside—but returns to the center at least once a week. "The people living and working outside usually take part in encounter sessions on their return visits," Ferrigno says. "Although they have to come back only once a week, most of them come back more often than that to try to help the other people in the program."

Since it is a voluntary program, an addict may drop out any time he chooses. But the dropout rate has been remarkably low—only fourteen percent in the preliminary phases of the program and three percent in the latter stages. At this writing, there are two hundred persons taking part in the live-in phase of the program and forty-five in the induction phase. Twenty-five addicts have completed the entire rehabilitation program, but several times that number are scheduled to complete it within a few months.

The SERA program for community development and organization has numerous functions. "Among other things, we provide what we call a political orientation service—getting people in from the community and educating them about things like who their congressman is or who their state senator is," Ferrigno explains. "We also have a referral service that helps people in the community find out what agencies are available to help them. We have a community action program in which a young woman from our staff attends all meetings of community organizations to keep us posted on what is going on in this area. Another of our programs is called Volunteers of SERA; it provides an eighteen-week course on drug abuse to volunteers, who then work in the community to prevent use of narcotics. We have a job development and placement service for former addicts taking part in our program. We also have a legal service to handle the addicts' problems with the courts; almost every addict involved in our program has some kind of criminal charges pending against him. Finally, we have a service that provides speakers and films on drug abuse to schools, community organizations, and so forth."

SERA's youth component is in its infancy at this writing. "It caters to kids eighteen years old and younger who've been experimenting with drugs but aren't hooked yet," Ferrigno says. "They live at home, but attend encounter groups, motivation sessions, and things like ceramics classes that try to channel their energies away from drugs to something constructive."

As an offshoot of SERA, Frank Gracia founded a separate organization composed of military veterans who became heroin addicts or continued their addiction while in the service. The veterans' organization is named Drug-Mending Zone, but more popularly known as DMZ. It works on the same general principles as SERA, and currently uses SERA's facilities, but is eventually scheduled to move into its own building nearby on East 167th Street. Originally, SERA accepted veterans in its program and handled them in much the same manner as other addicts. But by the middle of 1971, Gracia concluded that the veterans presented special problems and needed an organization of their own. "We found that the veterans can't relate well to street addicts," Gracia says. "They don't have the initiative of the street addict, and they didn't get hooked for the same reasons."

On Veterans Day, 1971, the sixty-two members of DMZ had a dinner in the SERA building at 1014 Hoe Avenue to celebrate the successful completion of the first three months of their program. Their relatives and girlfriends were allowed to attend. The mood was jubilant. After the veterans and their guests finished the meal—which included turkey, Caribbean salad, and fruit drinks prepared by the DMZ members themselves—the tables were pushed back and dancing began to a Latin beat thumped out on a set of bongos. Amid the noise, one mother sat against a wall and held her son's hand. A young veteran gestured animatedly to his girlfriend, trying to make himself heard above the din.

In an adjoining room, several of the DMZ members explained to visitors how they got involved in the program and how it was helping them. "I got addicted in the army," said Francisco Rivera, twenty-five, who spent two years in Vietnam. He returned home with a Silver Star, three Bronze Stars, four Purple Hearts, and a fifty-dollar-a-day heroin habit. He found himself ill-equipped to deal with the deceits of Hunts Point drug pushers, who robbed and beat him and sold him packets that were supposed to contain heroin but actually contained imitations such as ordinary flour. In a matter of weeks, Rivera said, he ran through two thousand dollars he had saved while in the army. Unable to obtain heroin, he turned himself in at a hospital and asked to be detoxified.

"They had me on methadone for three days," he said. "Then they cut me off [from methadone]. I couldn't take it, and I went out on the streets again." Later, still unable to kick the habit or adjust to the life of a street addict, he took the advice of a nun from a neighborhood church and sought help from SERA. He then was placed in DMZ, and was making significant progress toward rehabilitation.

Another DMZ member, Frank Arthur, a twenty-two-year-old Marine veteran, entered the program while on probation in an armed-robbery case. Arthur said he wanted to "get into the people business" when his rehabilitation was completed. "I saw how people helped me and I want to do the same," he said. "I'll stick with DMZ and become a counselor."

Frank Gracia, speaking of both the SERA and DMZ programs, says: "It's taken a lot of work, but we're rolling now. We're providing realistic programs and, if the money holds out, we'll be OK." Money is a problem. After operating on a $1.3-million budget its first year, SERA's expanded operations caused Gracia to ask the state for $1.7 million for the second year. The state rejected the request. For its second year, using money obtained from both state and city agencies, SERA's budget remained at $1.3 million.

"The fiscal irresponsibility up there [in the state government] is amazing," Gracia complains. "How the hell can they expect us to turn people away?" Gracia laments that there are hundreds of addicts in the streets he can't reach. He knows two brothers aged nine and eleven, for example, who are heroin addicts. The nine-year-old, who occasionally drops by Gracia's office, has been arrested forty-two times. "If that kid's living at twelve years of age, it's a miracle," Gracia says. (The minimum age for admission to SERA is thirteen.) "Kids like that around here, they're sentenced to die, man."

As for Lena T. and Alberto R., it is too early at this writing to know how successful they'll be in trying to kick the habit. But it is clear that they genuinely want to do so, and that may be more than half the battle—enough to get them a reprieve from the death sentence described by Frank Gracia.

Obviously, there is no single "villain" re- **11**
sponsible for the deplorable conditions in
Hunts Point. There is no question that
some of the victims of these conditions—
the people living in Hunts Point—are themselves
among the "villains." Many of them, even those
who complain most loudly about the filth and
crime and hopelessness of the ghetto, are among
the chief contributors to the continued deterioration of the
neighborhood. They do, as critics charge, deface their own
homes and those of their neighbors. They do ignore or con-
done acts of delinquency committed by their children. They
do, in some cases, take the easy way out by failing even to seek
work and relying on welfare payments to feed, clothe, and
house themselves and their families. They do often isolate
themselves and refuse to join in community efforts to improve
Hunts Point.

But, as serious as are the sins of omission and commission
perpetrated by residents of Hunts Point, those perpetrated by
the forces of government seem even greater. In short, government bureaucracy appears to be the most heinous "villain" of the Hunts Point piece.

Besides the examples of city government indifference cited
in Chapter Eight—such as those involving juvenile homes,
the Hunts Point Terminal Market, and hospital services—

countless other cases point up the callous disregard of Hunts Point's needs exhibited by officials at all levels of government. There is, for example, the question of how to rid Hunts Point of rats. The New York City Health Department is currently conducting a $4.3-million-a-year rat-eradication program aimed at five slum areas, including Hunts Point. Although the program is administered by the city, $2 million of its annual budget comes from the federal government and $1 million from the state government.

There are about 2,000 square blocks within the five target areas—including 368 in Hunts Point and adjoining sections of the South Bronx—but the eradication program's main thrust is aimed at only 500. Thus, three out of four blocks in Hunts Point and the other slum areas are being ignored, at least for the time being. A case can be made that every program has to start somewhere and can't possibly cover all necessary areas at once. But there are other failings in the eradication program.

The chief failing is that, at the very time the bureaucracy is supposedly trying to eliminate rats by poisoning them, it is simultaneously doing only a half-hearted job of collecting garbage—thus giving rats places to feed and thrive. The eradication program includes provisions for special garbage pickups in the most rat-infested areas. But they are made for brief periods, then abandoned. And in other sections the garbage pickups are even less regular. Throughout Hunts Point, residents complain steadily about overflowing trash cans, vacant lots and abandoned buildings filled with refuse, and streets strewn with litter.

Robert Nuñoz, an organizer for an antipoverty agency called the Hunts Point Community Corporation, says he gets at least thirty-five complaints a week from persons reporting that their garbage has not been collected. "We have to threaten the city with trouble before they'll pick up the garbage," he says. Although garbage is collected as often as six times a week in many sections of the city, Hunts Pointers say they are lucky if theirs is picked up twice a week. Johnny Melendez, deputy director of the Hunts Point Community Corporation, says: "We have to take the garbage and burn it in the streets because there are too many rats over here."

Occasionally, an important city official makes a tour of Hunts Point to get a firsthand look at the area's problems. Invariably, just before his visit, the City Sanitation Department exerts extra effort to pick up the garbage and make the neighborhood look as presentable as possible. Such was the case with a recent visit made by Jerome Kretchmer, head of the City Environmental Protection Administration, which includes the sanitation department. Just before his arrival, sanitation workers emptied the trash cans in the neighborhood—thus enabling Kretchmer to pronounce: "The garbage pickups aren't too bad around here."

But the fact was that, except for the emptying of the cans, little had been done to remove the piles of smelly garbage from Hunts Point. Abandoned buildings, vacant lots, and gutters remained cluttered. During his tour, Kretchmer made an impromptu visit to the headquarters of the Young Lords at Kelly Street and Longwood Avenue. Carlos Aponte, the Lords' education lieutenant, then led him through some of the more squalid spots in Hunts Point—showing him the tons of garbage that had been left behind by the sanitation workers.

"The people don't believe the city will do anything after you've gone and the publicity dies down," Aponte told Kretchmer. "Have you been into the back yards of some of these buildings?" Aponte asked, pointing to tenements on Kelly Street whose yards were piled high with garbage. "You have to wear a gas mask."

Kretchmer did inspect one such yard, where the odor was overpowering. He then told Aponte that the sanitation department could not enter such yards to clean them until the

City Health Department certified them as hazards. health department, while carrying on its $4.3-million program to eradicate rats, had failed to certify most yards in Hunts Point as hazards. Thus, the rats continued to feed and breed there. But Kretchmer conceded that even certifying the yards wouldn't necessarily solve the problem. "Once they are certified, we don't have anywhere near enough crews to do the cleanup," he said. He could not promise that anything would be done to remedy the situation.

Thus, when he left, the impression gathered by many Hunts Point residents was that Kretchmer's visit represented merely another example of the city making a show of interest in Hunts Point while continuing to neglect its problems. There was only one minor consolation. As Aponte gazed around at the yards and abandoned buildings filled with garbage, his eyes fell on the trash cans that had been emptied just before Kretchmer's arrival. "This is the cleanest this street has been in six months," he said. A few days later, however, the street was as garbage-strewn as ever.

Another way in which the bureaucracy is responsible for perpetuating intolerable conditions in Hunts Point is through the city's ownership of slum buildings. When a landlord abandons a ghetto building because he no longer finds it profitable and does not want to pay the taxes on it, the city usually takes over. Often, as has been pointed out previously, the city declares the building unfit for human habitation but permits the tenants to stay on and pay token rents. In other cases, the city takes over slum buildings by condemnation in preparation for public works projects and allows tenants to remain temporarily. Throughout Hunts Point, there are dilapidated buildings owned by the city.

Conditions in many such buildings are abysmal—even worse than in buildings owned by profiteering private slumlords. As a result, the city itself is getting the reputation of being a slumlord.

Recently, the directors of several urban-renewal projects complained that official neglect was causing thousands of tenants in city-owned buildings "severe and unwarranted hardships." The complaint, contained in a letter sent to City Housing and Development Administrator Albert A. Walsh, likened the city's practices to those "perpetrated by New York's worst slumlords." The letter added: "We can take you into any of our areas and introduce you to tenants who are frequently without heat or hot water in the middle of wintertime, live in fear of fire because electrical wiring isn't repaired, and find it impossible to get a broken toilet fixed or broken windows repaired."

Walsh conceded that conditions in the city-owned buildings were substandard. "That's why we acquired the buildings in the first place," he said. "It's a tough, dirty job to keep them up. We do the very best we can." But many tenants insisted that the conditions deteriorated markedly after the city took over the buildings.

"These guys [city employees] are as much plumbers as I am," said one tenant, Phalathers Gonzales. "They came in to fix the sink and knocked the wall loose. Then they came to fix the wall and knocked through the ceiling." Another tenant, William Allen, said: "It's never been great here, but we always had heat until the city started monkeying around."

Walsh and other officials were also assailed by other critics for allowing scandals to develop in the municipal loan program, under which owners of apartment buildings in Hunts Point were among those accused of bilking the city of hundreds of thousands of dollars. The program provided loans to the owners, ostensibly for renovation of slum buildings. In some cases, the repairs were never made or were made shoddily—but city inspectors were bribed to certify that the renovations had been satisfactorily completed. In other cases, landlords defaulted on their loan repayments to the city while continuing to collect rents from their tenants. In still others, the owners received inflated loans by submitting false statements on their financial situations to the city.

The chairman of a City Council investigating committee charged in one case that two brothers who obtained $3,376,000 to renovate eight Hunts Point buildings were continuing to collect rents while failing to repay the loans and interest. The chairman, Councilman Edward L. Sadowsky, said landlords Melvin and Gerald Weintraub had falllen into arrears totaling $214,557 on the repayments. At a hearing conducted by Sadowsky's committee, City Investigation Commissioner Robert K. Ruskin accused the brothers of obtaining $427,000 more in loans than they should have been allowed. He said they received the additional money by inflating the amounts of mortgages they claimed existed on some of their buildings and by listing one mortgage that did not exist at all.

The Weintraubs' Hunts Point buildings were all in the 900 block of Fox Street, one of the most dilapidated and drug-ridden streets in the area. Councilman Sadowsky said: "It is unconscionable that these developers should be able to reap the fruits of transactions in which the city was defrauded at the inception." He urged Mayor Lindsay to take "immediate steps to appoint receivers for these properties and place them in foreclosure." But a spokesman for the mayor said foreclosure would mean that "the city loses all hopes of recouping any losses incurred through previous transactions on that property." He said city lawyers were "thus working on a proposal to establish trusteeships for collecting rentals and depositing them in special accounts, out of which maintenance and debt service payments would be made." In the meantime, tenants in the Hunts Point buildings were obliged to continue making rent payments to the landlords—even if promised renovations were not made. When the Weintraubs refused to sign waivers of immunity in a criminal investigation, the city acted to ban them for five years from doing further municipal business.

In another case arising from the same scandal, the two owners of a Hunts Point building at 1411 Stebbins Avenue were indicted on charges of stealing $25,000 from the city by falsely claiming there was a mortgage on the building in that amount. The owners, Richard Braun and Jack Fried, were accused of obtaining a $25,000 loan from the city—ostensibly to satisfy the mortgage. Braun and Fried pleaded not guilty and were released without being required to post bail. Their trial is still pending at this writing.

When the scandal rose to the surface in 1971, Councilman Sadowsky charged that the basic facts in the affair were known by city officials two years earlier but that they had taken no effective corrective action. If a report on the alleged irregularities compiled in 1969 had not been "stuck away with no constructive action, we could have saved considerable grief and money and prevented criminal activities," Sadowsky said at a committee hearing. "The greater tragedy is that, so far as I can see, no effective action has been taken yet to avert further abuses. Housing and Development Administration officials don't seem to have grasped their problems yet."

Sadowsky sharply questioned William D. Clarke, who had been head of the municipal loan program at the time the 1969 report was compiled. He repeatedly asked Clarke why one irregularity or another disclosed in the report from the loan program's inspector general had not been corrected. Clarke replied variously that there had been insufficient personnel, that he had "taken steps," that a particular case cited was "an isolated one," or "that was not my responsibility."

In exasperation, Sadowsky finally shouted: "All of a sudden in 1971 different investigations swooped down, there's a whole to-do, indictments, and here back in May, 1969, the inspector general says the problem is there—it's going to happen. How do you account for the fact that nothing was done until what developed in these indictments?"

Clarke replied: "Let's not say nothing was done. There was a drastic exchange of memoranda." In the view of numerous Hunts Pointers, many of their problems with the city government stem from the fact that there are too many exchanges of memoranda by officials and too little action.

Some of their problems, however, stem from the hamstringing of antipoverty programs designed to help them—hamstringing caused by friction between poverty agency leaders in Hunts Point and officials of the city, state, and federal governments. A prime example involved the Hunts Point Multi-Service Center Corporation, a major antipoverty agency in the area. Established in 1968, the center is designed to provide health, job placement, housing, economic development, and youth service programs. Most of its funds are provided by the federal government, but it is subject to supervision by both federal and city officials.

In the spring of 1970 the head of the center, Ramon S. Velez, took a leave of absence to run against five other candidates for the Democratic nomination for a congressional seat. The nomination and election were subsequently won by Herman Badillo. Following his unsuccessful campaign, Velez charged, he and the center began to be subjected to "harassment" and restrictions by various federal and city officials. He completely absolved Congressman Badillo of any role in the purported harassment, saying Badillo had supported him and the work of the center. "Somebody somewhere may feel we have grown too fast," Velez said, in seeking to explain the problems with public officials.

The officials, meanwhile, denied there had been any harassment. They said the problems were the making of Velez and his associates at the antipoverty center. Of the $12 million allocated to the center from 1968 to 1970, the officials said, Velez and his aides could not account for how $1.6 million had been spent. As a result, S. William Green, regional administrator of the U.S. Department of Housing and Urban Development, ordered that further federal payments to the center from his agency be suspended, "at least temporarily." Federal and city investigations of the center's handling of funds were launched.

At the same time, however, other federal agencies such as the Department of Health, Education, and Welfare, the Labor Department, and the Office of Economic Opportunity continued to provide funds to the center. But the suspension of payments by the Department of Housing and Urban Development, plus the local and federal investigations, resulted in a severe cutback in services. Velez angrily denied that he or his associates had done anything wrong.

"We can account for every penny," he said. "All I asked for was time to produce the records. They are accusing us of not providing proper documentation, not of stealing anything." He said that, for a time, the center did not have qualified personnel handling accounting and purchasing matters. In addition, part of the problem arose because funds from various agencies were placed in the same account and could not be adequately traced as they were disbursed. Federal approval of contracts and disbursements of funds often came so late that the center was forced to use money from one agency for continuing programs approved by another, Velez said. He said he had been questioned by investigators about why he had received $5,000 pay in cash, instead of compensatory time off, for working extra hours. Sixty to seventy other employees of the center has also received such cash as a regular practice, Velez said. Velez's straight salary was $27,000 a year.

When federal officials asked him to submit weekly financial reports, Velez charged that the request was further evidence of harassment. He said the request was unfair and impossible to fulfill. As a result, he offered to resign. But the center's board of directors unanimously rejected the resignation.

Later, it was revealed that, because of the delays by various agencies in providing promised funds, the center had failed to pay $675,000 in federal, state, and city taxes. Meanwhile, the U.S. Department of Housing and Urban Development continued to hold up funds for the center. Velez threatened to shut the center down during the summer of 1971, but eventually was persuaded to keep the program going on a reduced budget. The center's staff dropped from 500 to 350, and services were sharply curtailed.

But finally, in November, 1971, an agreement was reached under which $4 billion in federal funds were released to the center and new financial controls were put in effect. The agreement provided for the City Human Resources Administration to receive grants from the federal government, then pass the funds on to the center and monitor their use. A senior specialist from the city agency, Ismael Quiles, was named to serve as a management-fiscal consultant at the center. He was assigned to develop a new budget, oversee all checks drawn, and develop controls on purchasing, personnel, and the like. In addition, an outside management and accounting firm was chosen by the city and the center to make fiscal recommendations, arrange payment of back taxes, and set up an improved system for keeping records.

At the same time the dispute was raging over the Hunts Point Multi-Service Center Corporation, another antipoverty agency in Hunts Point was having its own problems. The hiring practices of the agency, the Hunts Point Community Corporation, were under investigation by Bronx District Attorney Burton Roberts and a grand jury. The community corporation, among other things, operated a Neighborhood

Youth Corps program in Hunts Point with funds provided by the federal and city governments. Under the program, about 1,800 teen-agers were hired for summer jobs in such fields as community service and hospital work. The aim was to provide actual work experience, rather than job training.

The problem arose when it was discovered that many of the youths hired apparently were technically ineligible for the jobs. Under federal regulations, those hired were supposed to come from families whose total incomes were below the poverty level. A federal index sets the poverty level for a family of four, for example, at $3,200 a year. Although almost all of the youths hired came from disadvantaged families, many of them were above the poverty level.

In the end, the grand jury declined to indict anyone—pointing out in a report that many of the enrollment forms for the program were filled out by youngsters who signed their parents' names or were signed by parents who had no idea of what they were signing. The grand jury report also urged that the federal poverty index be raised to account for higher living costs in New York than in other parts of the country. "It is clear that a national poverty index, while admittedly simple to promulgate, cannot sufficiently reflect the economic pressures and cost of living for every locality," the report said. "New York City, with its high cost of living and serious housing shortage, cannot be held to a standard adequate for San Diego, California, or Jackson, Mississippi." The grand jury also recommended that the U.S. Labor Department provide financing for the Neighborhood Youth Corps program early in the year, rather than early in the summer, to avoid last-minute enrollment procedures; that parents' signatures on application papers be notarized; and that better communication be established among antipoverty agencies.

District Attorney Roberts said the purpose of the recommendations was to "help correct a fine program rather than to punish individuals for violating the laws." But the fact was that the investigation placed a cloud over the work of the antipoverty agency and threw a scare into many of the youngsters who had been given summer jobs. It also reinforced the belief of numerous Hunts Pointers—whether justified or unjustified—that the machinery of government was designed in such a way that it served more as a detriment to their interests than as a benefit.

Another incident that pointed up Hunts Pointers' suspicion of bureaucracy involved a welfare recipient, Mrs. Luz Maria Diaz. She had been receiving welfare payments of $133.70 a month. Mrs. Diaz reported to welfare workers that one of her checks had been lost or undelivered, so another check was issued in its place. Later, the City Department of Social Services claimed the second check had been "improperly issued." As a result, the department notified Mrs. Diaz that, in the future, her checks would be reduced to $122.35 to compensate for the check that had supposedly been issued improperly. Many another welfare recipient, after receiving such a notice from the Department of Social Services, had meekly accepted the decision. But Mrs. Diaz decided to fight.

She asked for help from Hunts Point Legal Services, a federally financed agency that provides lawyers for indigent Hunts Pointers. The agency filed a suit against city and state welfare officials, demanding that Mrs. Diaz and all other welfare clients faced with termination or modification of their benefits be given "fair hearings" at the state level before such changes could take effect. This contention was later upheld by State Supreme Court Justice Samuel A. Spiegel.

The judge ruled that the right to receive welfare benefits must be protected fully under the constitutional guarantee of due process of justice. "Welfare assistance is a matter of right and not merely a privilege or charity," Spiegel wrote. "The [U.S.] Supreme Court has clearly decreed that 'such benefits are a matter of statutory entitlement for persons qualified to receive them. Their termination or modification involves state action that adjudicates important basic rights.' "

To city officials' arguments that granting a "fair hearing" at the state level would impose massive administrative problems, the judge replied: "This is no answer to the constitutional rights to due process owed to the dissatisfied recipient. Nor is it so overwhelmingly compelling as to justify the slightest curtailment of a recipient's constitutional rights. . . . The 'fair hearing' directed by the state . . . must conform to all constitutional safeguards, irrespective of inconvenience or inexpediency."

Although Mrs. Diaz ultimately won her case in the courts, the affair left a sour taste in the mouths of many Hunts Pointers. It was typical, they said, of the arbitrary way in which the bureaucracy tried to deal with ghetto residents.

For balance, it should be pointed out that not all bureaucrats are indifferent to the plight of Hunts Pointers. Some government officials and employees are sincerely trying to improve conditions in the area. Often their efforts get bogged down by the cumbersome machinery of government. But sometimes they manage to "beat the system" and achieve worthwhile results.

In one such case, fifteen teams of health specialists moved into Hunts Point with mobile medical equipment to provide examinations and treatment from vans parked in the streets. Among their chief aims was to detect and treat lead poisoning in young children. As previously pointed out, many ghetto children have an abnormal taste for paint. They scrape the paint off walls of their homes and eat it. Continued eating of paint containing lead over a period of months can cause encephalitis (inflammation of the brain), with resulting brain damage, mental retardation, and even death.

The health teams—made up of doctors and nurses from

city hospitals, supported by personnel provided by the City Health Department Bureau of Lead Poisoning and the Hunts Point Community Corporation—found many children suffering from lead poisoning. One six-year-old girl was found to have a toxic level of lead in her blood. But because she was treated in time, her life was saved and she was spared any permanent ill effects. In preparation for the visits by the health teams, health department aides spent two weeks canvassing the neighborhood and making appointments for examinations. A soundtruck bearing the legend "Take the Lead Out" toured Hunts Point, alerting residents to the program.

In addition to checking for lead poisoning, the teams looked for symptoms of anemia, malnutrition, tuberculosis, and cancer, among other ailments. Their vans contained X-ray machines and equipment for conducting Pap tests to detect cancer of the cervix. The specialists measured and weighed all children examined to detect growth deficiencies. They also provided parents with advice on diets.

One five-year-old boy, Papo Rodriguez, took a look at a hypodermic needle a doctor planned to insert in his arm and screamed: "I don't want it. I don't want it." But Papo's father gently patted his head and told him: "You want it, son. You need it." Papo took it.

Dr. Simon Cohen, a pediatrician who devised the plan for sending the health teams into Hunts Point, said: "Lead poisoning is obviously not the most important problem facing this community. Compared with heroin, it's not one-thousandth as crucial. But when you think of the human cost of one child getting encephalitis, it's worth it."

Sometimes, all it takes is the imagination and extra effort of one person to provide Hunts Point with tangible benefits. One such person is Sylvia (Pat) Bean, the supervising librarian at the Hunts Point Library on Southern Boulevard. The library, built early in this century, had fallen into disrepair and relative disuse in recent years. But, when Miss Bean took over, she decided to convert it into a community resource whose value would extend far beyond the traditional concept of a neighborhood library. She organized rock concerts and talent shows for teen-agers at the library. She sponsored Christmas parties at which many Hunts Point children saw their first Christmas trees. She showed free movies and organized a poetry workshop run by black and Puerto Rican poets. Gradually, the young people and adults who started coming to the library for the other activities took an interest in the books, magazines and research materials as well.

Now, Miss Bean keeps the library open until ten P.M. four nights a week. She often works a twelve-hour day. A native of Bermuda and a former teacher, Miss Bean finds the extra effort bringing her the greatest rewards of her career. "What's important is what I accomplish," she says. "I'm happy if someone comes into my library just to get warm. Then I know I've made him welcome."

The same sort of imagination that can revitalize a library can also channel young people's interests from the destructive to the constructive. It will be recalled that, with the help of policemen from the 41st Precinct, members of a youth gang called the Ghetto Brothers were provided with a storefront to use as a headquarters. The Ghetto Brothers, in turn, abandoned their role as a fighting gang and began devoting much of their time to community service. In one case, for example, they helped representatives of the Mayor's Council on the Environment, the Parks Department, and school officials organize a project to clean up a debris-strewn section of Crotona Park East.

About two hundred school-age youngsters raked leaves, picked up soda cans and bottles, swept walks, and emptied wire baskets for an entire day. Members of the Ghetto Brothers both helped in the cleanup and entertained the youngsters while they worked—playing Latin music on a variety of instruments from a mobile stage provided by the Parks Department. Many of the youngsters also brought with them from home large plastic bags filled with empty aluminum cans that were collected at the park and put into a recycling truck. They were paid ten cents a pound for the cans, but the money seemed secondary to them.

One parent who accompanied his three sons to the park, Roberto Hernandez, said: "We've been saving the cans for a while. We want to do our part. There's no sense of dirtying the place if we're going to use it." Harold Press, a teacher from a nearby school who led a delegation of thirty students helping in the cleanup project, said: "They know why they're here. We've been talking about this for quite a while. We're determined to make this a decent place for play and relaxation."

When the cleanup was completed, a twelve-year-old boy, Luis Matos, summed it all up simply in six words. "It's nice," he said. "It has real meaning."

12

Samuel Doneifsky was born on July 1, 1880, in a small community on the outskirts of Kiev, Russia. He was a Jew, and times were hard for Jews in Russia. By and large, they were segregated in ghettoized communities such as the one where Sam grew up. They were discouraged from educating themselves. They were compelled to serve in the army, and usually given the most distasteful assignments the officers could find.

When Sam was twenty-three, he found himself in the army and hated it. He had a rebellious spirit that compelled him to tell off superiors he felt were discriminating against him. The more he rebelled, the more abuse they piled on him. Finally, Sam had all he could take. Resorting to a time-honored tradition in the Russian army, he paid a small bribe to a minor functionary and was given his discharge. He then decided to leave Russia and seek his fortune in America.

Making his way across Europe alone, he eventually reached Rotterdam, Holland, in January, 1904. He boarded a ship crowded with fellow immigrants on January 15, and arrived in New York on January 25. Once settled in a rooming house in Manhattan, he began working ceaselessly toward the goal of making enough money so that he could pay for the passage of his parents and other relatives from Russia to the United States.

Like many of his fellow immigrants, he found his first work in New York as a pushcart peddler—hawking produce on the Lower East Side. He saved enough money to become a partner in the first of a series of produce stores that he would eventually operate. By 1907, he had been able to bring his family to New York. He had also met and courted a beautiful, fair-skinned girl named Anna Wilder who lived with her parents just up the street from an apartment Sam had rented at 322 East 101st Street. Anna and her family had emigrated to the United States from Austria several years earlier. Anna was a cousin of Billy Wilder, who would later become a renowned motion-picture director and screenwriter.

At five P.M. on Sunday, February 10, 1907, Sam and Anna were married in an establishment known as Victoria Palace Hall at 227 East 98th Street. Anna was just sixteen; Sam was twenty-six. They set up housekeeping in the apartment on 101st Street and, ten months later, their first child was born—a son, named Arthur. Anna would later give birth to a daughter, named Lillian, and another son, named Henry. On June 22, 1909, Sam became an American citizen.

Sam's business prospered. In addition to selling produce at retail, he became a large-scale wholesale supplier. A religious Jew and something of a Biblical scholar, he was looking forward by 1919 to an important event—the bar mitzvah of his oldest son. For some time, he had contemplated buying a house. Now, he decided, was the time. The family could move into the house in time to celebrate Arthur's bar mitzvah with an elaborate party. The house he chose was a comfortable two-family brick home in Hunts Point, at 888 Irvine Street. Sam's family would live on the ground floor; Sam would rent the second-floor apartment.

The party in honor of Arthur's bar mitzvah was the first of many huge family gatherings that were to take place in the house during the next four decades. Relatives and friends from throughout the New York area—and some from as far off as Hartford, Connecticut—descended on Irvine Street for the occasion. Over the years, the house would become a "family home"—open to any relative or friend who needed a temporary place to stay or a home-cooked meal. After Billy Wilder fled from Nazi Germany, where he had been a newspaperman and movie-maker, he went first to Paris and then to the United States. He stayed for a time at the house on Irvine Street before heading for Hollywood. The ground floor of the house had seven rooms, plus an enclosed porch. But, in a pinch, it could accommodate a seemingly limitless number of persons.

One of the main attractions that lured visitors on the slightest pretext was Anna's bounteous dinner table. A superb cook and baker, she sometimes spent her summers supervising kitchen operations at Catskill Mountain resort hotels. One of her baking specialties was an incredibly light concoction made of frozen-dough pastry filled with sugar, nuts, and heaven-knows-what-else. She would never give anyone the precise recipe. "You put in a little sugar, a few nuts, some butter," she would say. Even after she let others watch the baking process, nobody could duplicate the process.

But, if she was stingy with her cooking secrets, Anna was more than generous with her food—constantly prompting guests to "eat, eat." No matter how much they argued that they were filled beyond capacity, she'd always plop another portion on their plates. She was, in this respect, perhaps, the Jewish mother carried to ridiculous extremes.

Behind the Irvine Street house was a large yard, where Sam planted pear and cherry trees. When the cherries ripened, he picked them and carried them to the basement—then left them to ferment into a sweet, potent wine. In time, much of the basement was filled with wine barrels. Special guests were given bottles of wine to take home.

During the winters, a favorite pastime of Hunts Point children was coasting down hills on sleds. The more adventurous youngsters used a steep hill on Seneca Avenue, running from Faile Street toward the Bronx River. But Sam and Anna put the Seneca Avenue hill off limits to their children, feeling it was too steep and too heavily traveled for safety. Despite the ban, Henry occasionally made secret swoops down the hill on his Flexible Flyer.

Even after all three of their children had married, Sam and Anna maintained the Irvine Street house as a "family home." At one time or another, all three of the children, their spouses, and sons shared the house with Sam and Anna. But by the early 1950's, as the beginning of the deterioration became apparent, the children (who had by that time moved away) urged their parents to sell the house. Sam repeatedly refused. This was his home, and nobody was going to drive him out of it. Real-estate blockbusters tried to scare him into a panic sale, but Sam was not one to panic. He was still very active, in the produce business and private life, and he feared no man. By that time, Sam had become known as one of the best judges of produce quality in New York. About dusk of every working day, he left home—carrying a small hatchet—and went by subway to the railroad docks where produce was unloaded. Using his hatchet, he would pry open a crate or two of various types of produce. Then, on the basis of examining a few samples, he might buy as much as whole carloads of merchandise. He would not return home until midmorning, when he would go to bed and sleep through most of the daylight hours.

Because of Sam's working hours, Anna was left alone in the house at night—a problem that became increasingly acute as Hunts Point became ever more crime-ridden. Still, Sam refused to sell the house. During the mid-1950's, Sam retired. He spent most of his time in the house, watching television and reading. (His favorite reading matter was the

Yiddish daily newspaper published in New York, the *Forward*.) He watched with dismay as one after another of his neighbors moved away, to be replaced by newcomers with dark skins. As he walked the streets on occasional shopping excursions, he found nobody with whom to pause and pass the time of day. He felt almost a stranger in the neighborhood he had loved for almost forty years. Finally, with sad resignation, he sold the house. He and Anna moved to an apartment on Sheridan Avenue in the West Bronx, a few blocks from Yankee Stadium.

There, when friends and relatives came to visit, he continued to tell the corny old jokes he had told for years on Irvine Street. Sample: "If you eat potatoes for a hundred years, you'll live to be an old man." Sam ate potatoes for seventy-eight years. He died on April 1, 1959, two months short of his seventy-ninth birthday. Anna outlived him by almost six years, dying at the age of seventy-five on March 26, 1965.

Today, the quarters at 888 Irvine Street formerly occupied by Sam, Anna, and their family are occupied by Mrs. Elisa Torres and her family. Compared with other buildings in Hunts Point, time has been relatively kind to the house. It seems to be in better condition than many of its neighbors. Its dark bricks have been covered recently with whitewash. And, although the formerly grassy area of the back yard has been replaced by cement, Sam's pear and apple trees remain.

Sharing the ground-floor apartment with Elisa Torres are five of her seven children—Thelma, twenty-three; Nelson, twenty; Edgar, seventeen; Jose, fifteen; and Madeleine, twelve—and Thelma's one-year-old son, Alex. There are parallels between the story of Elisa's family and the story of Sam's family. Just as Sam emigrated from Russia and earned enough money to bring his family to New York, Elisa emigrated from Puerto Rico and made enough to bring her family, one by one, to New York.

"We're originally from P.R.—from Ponce," says Elisa's son Nelson. "About ten years ago, my mother left there because we couldn't make enough money there. She came to New York and got a job in a restaurant. When she could afford it, she started bringing one of us at a time to New York. My father—his name is Raymond—stayed behind because he can't stand the cold weather here in the winter. But he comes and stays with us in the summer."

At first, the family lived in an apartment house on West Farms Road in the Bronx. But, as the group in New York expanded, more space was needed and Elisa rented the ground floor of the Irvine Street house. She pays the landlord $185 a month, a high rent for Hunts Point. "Yeah, it's high," Nelson says. "But it's not too hard for us to pay. I work in a restaurant and Thelma works, too, and we put our money toward the rent."

Although the occupants have changed, the home is still very much a "family house." It is kept clean. The furniture is attractive and relatively new. Outside, the front stoop and the sidewalk are neatly swept. Although there may be filth and depressing conditions in the surrounding area, they are not present in this house.

Elisa and her children have formed casual acquaintance-ships with several of their Puerto Rican neighbors. But they have no close friends in the neighborhood. And they do not even know Hazel Fleming (see Chapter One), who lives in a private house directly across the street from them.

Jose attends James Monroe High School, Edgar attends Maritime Trades High School in Manhattan, and Madeleine goes to Junior High School 125. In their spare time, Nelson and his brothers and sisters usually go bowling or go to the Spanish-language movies on Southern boulevard.

Nelson draws a distinction between the section of Hunts Point where his family lives and other parts of the neighborhood. "It's not too bad right around here," he told an interviewer. "This section is better than, say, the area around Simpson Street. The buildings are in better condition and people take better care of them. It's safer here, too. We haven't been robbed since we've lived here. Up near Simpson Street, there's narcotics all over the place. Here, there's some narcotics—but not as much. Here, there's some crime—but not as much, either."

While Nelson was being interviewed at his home, however, one or more thieves were stealing the battery from the interviewer's automobile—parked in broad daylight on a relatively busy street a half-block away.

13

Mrs. Sarah Wachtel is a short, attractive blonde who often goes to work wearing a semi-mini skirt and a pair of calf-length boots. She looks as if she might be a successful businesswoman, perhaps a buyer for a chic department store. If there is one typical image that she does not seem to fit, it is that of a school principal. All of which goes to show that appearances can indeed be deceiving, for Mrs. Wachtel is the principal of P.S. 48.

Although the problems of running a ghetto school are formidable, Mrs. Wachtel has a knack for seeing the bright side of a situation. Yes, she says, P.S. 48 is in a decaying neighborhood. Yes, there are drugs and crime and all sorts of other troubles. But the section surrounding the school is not the most depressed area in Hunts Point by any means. As did Nelson Torres, Mrs. Wachtel points out that the section near Simpson Street, for example, is far worse.

"I like to think of our section as the beginning of upward mobility in Hunts Point," she says. "The people here have a little more money and are living in a little better places than those in other parts of Hunts Point. From here, they may move to better neighborhoods."

In some ways, however, this slightly higher status—and it

is so slight that it is almost imperceptible to some—works to the detriment of the area's residents and the students at P.S. 48. Since other sections of Hunts Point are considered worse than the area in the immediate vicinity of the school, those sections receive the bulk of the antipoverty aid. "This is a forgotten area," Mrs. Wachtel says. "Since we're fairly close to the Hunts Point Market and some other business places, government agencies consider this an industrial area. They treat it as if it doesn't need the services that residential poverty areas get. But this is very much a residential area. We've got twenty-two hundred students in this school, so you know there have to be plenty of people living around here. We're minus all the agencies we need—health agencies, social agencies, and so forth. The only social agency in this area is this school."

Mrs. Wachtel has been principal of P.S. 48 since 1968, and before that was assistant principal for eleven years. Thus she has witnessed much of the transformation that has taken place in Hunts Point. "When I came here, the pupil population of this school was approximately fifty percent middle-class Jewish," she says. "The area was in the process of change, but the mass influx of Puerto Ricans and blacks hadn't taken place. Now, sixty-three percent of our students are Puerto Rican, thirty-two percent are black, and only five percent are white—mostly from Italian or Greek families."

The language barrier confronting many Puerto Rican students is a major obstacle, and Mrs. Wachtel concedes that her staff is ill-equipped to deal with it. "About one hundred to one hundred twenty-five children come into the school every year without being able to speak virtually any English at all," she says. "Many of the others speak just a smattering of English." Yet the school has only one bilingual teacher. "Unfortunately, we haven't been able to recruit bilingual teachers," Mrs. Wachtel says. She tries to alleviate the situation by employing fifty-five paraprofessionals—teachers' aides and the like—many of whom speak Spanish. But they are no substitute for qualified bilingual teachers.

Part of the problem in trying to recruit bilingual teachers —and other teachers as well—is that potential faculty members are afraid to venture into Hunts Point. "Here's a perfect example," Mrs. Wachtel says. "A friend of mine is teaching an education course at Lehman College. She tried to get one of her classes to visit our school, to see what it was like and what we were doing here. Her students heard 'Hunts Point' and all they could think about were drugs, crime, and rape. They told her they were afraid they'd be attacked here or that their cars would be stolen. They refused to come, so the visit was canceled."

The staff at P.S. 48 takes pains to try to instill in the students a sense of ethnic pride. In a hallway outside Mrs. Wachtel's office, for example, there are several bulletin boards covered with displays describing the accomplishments of Negroes and Puerto Ricans. One board bears the legend: "We Are Proud of Our Black Americans." Beneath it are pictures and brief biographies of such persons as James Baldwin, Louis Armstrong, Sidney Poitier, Leontyne Price, Arthur Ashe, Whitney Young, Jr., and Bill Russell. Another board bears the jackets of books with such titles as *Puerto Rican and Proud* and *Puerto Rico Workbook*. This board also points out the importance to Puerto Rican students of learning English. Under the heading "The Magic of English," it displays some of the tools used in teaching English. These include English and Spanish editions of the same books, such as *Aqui Viene El Ponchado* (a baseball novel whose English title is *Here Comes the Strikeout*) and *Danielito y el Dinosauro* (*Danny and the Dinosaur*).

Still another bulletin board extols the virtues of good citizenship. It bears pictures of various P.S. 48 students whose activities have been praised by their teachers as examples of

Americanism at its best. This board is decorated with a picture of a spacecraft and the motto: "Good Citizenship—Rocket to Success."

But it takes more than slogans and bulletin boards to accomplish tangible results in a ghetto school. Mrs. Wachtel and members of her staff have ventured far beyond the confines of usual faculty activities in attempts to win the confidence of the community and bring about improved conditions at P.S. 48. The school was opened in 1916, and much of its equipment is antiquated. It was designed for far fewer students than it now accommodates. For several years, parents and staff members pleaded with city officials to relieve the overcrowding and provide the school with better equipment. They got many promises, but no action. "One time, we even went down to City Hall and met with the mayor's educational liaison man," Mrs. Wachtel recalls. "He gave us a written promise that we'd be provided with additional classroom space. But still nothing happened."

At that point, Mrs. Wachtel and her teachers led several boycotts of the school, in which parents and students cooperated fully. During one such boycott, which lasted three days, the faculty, parents, and students picketed the Hunts Point Market to protest that the city had spent millions of dollars there while ignoring the needs of the school. Mrs. Wachtel concedes that the picketing of the market was an attention-getting device, designed to attract publicity. It succeeded. Each day, Mrs. Wachtel says, the picketing was filmed by television crews and aired on the evening newscasts. "Every night, when I'd get home, my husband would ask me: 'Can we eat dinner now or do we have to wait until the news is over?'"

The publicity achieved what years of personal appeals had not. City officials agreed to provide P.S. 48 with several "mini-schools"—portable classrooms in the shape of house-trailers—that were placed in a school yard formerly used as a play area. Even they, however, did not entirely remedy the space problem. Under continued pressure, the city officials ultimately agreed to build an additional elementary school in the neighborhood within the next few years.

Because of the faculty's close cooperation with parents on such matters as the boycotts, Mrs. Wachtel says, "We have a very positive community image." Unlike the atmosphere at some other schools in ghetto areas, she says, there is no hostility between the staff and the community. Despite the problems posed by living in the neighborhood, she feels many of her students' parents don't care to move away because they want their children to continued attending P.S. 48. "Sometimes, when people do move, they even falsify their addresses [to school officials] so their children can keep coming here," Mrs. Wachtel points out.

From all indications, the staff at P.S. 48 is succeeding to a greater degree than the staffs at various other schools in Hunts Point and nearby areas of the South Bronx in overcoming the problems of providing education in a ghetto. One such indication was provided by the results of reading tests given in all schools in New York City. While the scores of P.S. 48 students were generally well below the national average, as expected, they were at the same time generally higher than the scores of students in other nearby schools. For example, the median score among fifth-graders at P.S. 48 was 4.6—equivalent to what would be expected nationally of a student in his sixth month of the fourth grade. The national median score for fifth graders was 5.7, meaning P.S. 48 students were generally more than a year behind the norm. But most students at other schools in Hunts Point and the South Bronx were even farther behind. P.S. 75 at Faile Street and Bruckner Boulevard, the Hunts Point elementary school closest to P.S. 48, produced a median fifth-grade score of 3.6— a full year behind the result of P.S. 48. The average of fifth-grade results in eighteen schools throughout the South Bronx was 4.0. Other yardsticks also show students at P.S. 48 achieving better results than students at many other schools in the area.

But this does not, by any means, diminish the very serious problems existing at the school. The accomplishments at P.S. 48 can be viewed as successes only when measured against other ghetto schools. When compared with typical American schools outside ghetto areas, P.S. 48 is far behind. "We've been designated a poverty-pocket school," Mrs. Wachtel says. "That means we meet all the criteria required to receive special federal antipoverty funds. The criteria include such things as how many children we have who are entitled to receive free lunches at school, how much student mobility there is—that is, how many children move into and out of our area every year—and so forth." Thus, despite Mrs. Wachtel's assessment that the area surrounding P.S. 48 is in slightly better condition than some other sections of Hunts Point, the fact remains that it meets all the requisites of a slum.

At the same time, although P.S. 48 qualifies for federal antipoverty funds, Mrs. Wachtel contends that the area in the vicinity of the school is being wrongfully deprived of a great deal of additional aid. "This area should be getting a lot of funds under the Model Cities program but it's not," she says. "This area is excluded from the Model Cities program. It's just another example of this being a forgotten area."

(Although the federal Model Cities program includes a major portion of Hunts Point, it does not include the section near P.S. 48. Mrs. Wachtel says the reason for the exclusion was, as in the case of other antipoverty programs, that the section near the school was mistakenly designated by government agencies as an industrial area. The Model Cities program was begun in 1967 as a "massive assault on the physical, social, and economic problems" of American slums. Among the programs it provides in the South Bronx,

[163]

including the parts of Hunts Point that are covered, are a college scholarship program, a summer camp program, a drug-abuse program, and an economic development program.)

In describing conditions in the area near P.S. 48 as a notch better than those in some other sections of Hunts Point, Mrs. Wachtel does not minimize the problems that are nonetheless present. "Look, we've got crime and drugs and everything else here," she says. "We don't deny that. But there seems to be less of it than in other parts of Hunts Point. What disturbs us is that we get lumped in with all the other sections in the public's mind and people think it's as bad here as over near Simpson Street."

In some other Hunts Point elementary schools, it is not at all uncommon for teachers and administrators to discover students are heroin addicts. At P.S. 48, Mrs. Wachtel says, not one child has been definitely identified as an addict. "Of course, that doesn't necessarily mean we don't have any," she says. "It's very difficult to prove—unless a child is an obvious mainliner. We do know of some children in this school who come from families where there are older brothers and sisters or parents who are addicts."

Why is it that P.S. 48 seems to be succeeding to a greater extent than most other Hunts Point schools? One clue to the answer appears to lie in the very fact that conditions in the area are slightly better than in other sections of the ghetto. The residents are a trifle better off economically, perhaps slightly better educated themselves than other Hunts Pointers, and therefore are more apt to have children who come to school with a small head start over their fellow ghetto students.

(The reasons for the slightly better conditions around P.S. 48 are chiefly geographic. The school is in the southeast section of the neighborhood—the area where the Hunt, Jessup, and Richardson families originally settled in the seventeenth century. This section, closer to the East and Bronx Rivers than are other parts of Hunts Point, is the most isolated from the remainder of the Bronx. When poor black and Puerto Rican families began moving into Hunts Point, they made their first inroads at the opposite end of the neighborhood because it was closest to the sections from which they had come. Gradually, they moved ever farther south and east—toward the rivers. Thus, the migration came last to the section near P.S. 48. Partly because it remained in the hands of more affluent whites longer than did other sections, and partly because it had always contained somewhat higher-class housing than those sections, this area offered people forced to live in Hunts Point a slight upward step. Rents in the area were comparatively higher than in other sections of Hunts Point, so the tenants tended to be a bit more affluent —poor, to be sure, but not quite so poor as many other Hunts Pointers. It remains an open question, however, whether this section will retain its higher status. There is a strong possibility that, with the passage of a few more years, it will deteriorate to the point where it will be indistinguishable from the remainder of Hunts Point.)

The slightly better conditions in the area, however, do not provide the whole answer to the relative success of P.S. 48 in comparison with other Hunts Point schools. Another ingredient, much less tangible but nonetheless vital, is the tradition that has been built up at P.S. 48 over the years. During the period when Hunts Point had a small-town atmosphere, the school became a center of community activity. Far more than the typical New York City school or even other schools in the Hunts Point area, it developed close relationships among teachers, administrators, students, and parents that transcended the educational process. Years after their graduation, students would return to the school for frequent visits. The faculty stability—with many teachers remaining at P.S. 48 for a quarter-century or longer—tended to tighten still further the bonds between the school and the community. When the school observed its fiftieth anniversary, scores of former teachers and alumni—most of whom had long since left Hunts Point—returned for what Mrs. Wachtel calls a "gala celebration." Such an event might not be uncommon in a small town. In New York City these days, it is quite rare.

Although the small-town atmosphere and most of the long-time residents have left Hunts Point, the community spirit has been preserved at P.S. 48. It has been embraced by many of the new black and Puerto Rican residents, anxious to find some positive force in Hunts Point with which they can identify. Mrs. Wachtel's office is often filled with delegations of parents seeking help on problems beyond the scope of the school. To their credit, Mrs. Wachtel and her subordinates consider the solution of these problems part of their jobs. In the absence of necessary social agencies in the neighborhood, they feel the school must serve as a focus for community action on a broad range of issues.

Terms such as "tradition" and "community spirit" may seem corny and ethereal in reference to a neighborhood confronted with the monumental troubles that afflict Hunts Point. But they are clearly essential to the progress being shown at P.S. 48. And that progress represents one of the few hopeful signs in a generally dismal picture in Hunts Point.

14

Max Vogel is a short, frail merchant with an easy smile and a sense of resignation about the vicissitudes of life. For the last thirty-five years, he has owned the V&M Department store at 874 Hunts Point Avenue. The store's name is something of a misnomer; it is not a department store in the conventional sense, but rather a tiny shop that specializes chiefly in selling inexpensive clothing.

Max, who operates the store with his son, made a comfortable living there for many years. Hundreds of Hunts Pointers, with whom he maintained a first-name relationship, preferred doing business with him to shopping at larger stores elsewhere. There was never any question about a customer having satisfaction guaranteed at Max's store. If someone went home with a shirt and then decided he wanted a different style or color, he could return weeks later and still be allowed to exchange it. And it didn't matter if he'd lost the sales slip, either. Max knew all his customers and remembered everything he'd sold them.

Today, Max Vogel cannot make a living from his store. "Ah, nobody can make any money in Hunts Point any more," he says. "There's no business around here. The people don't have any money to spend—they're too poor. Fifteen years ago, this neighborhood had mostly Jewish, Irish, and Italian people. They worked hard, they made money and they could afford to spend money. Now, the people here are all colored or Puerto Rican. A lot of them are on welfare. And even those who aren't have no money to spend. Besides that, some of them will steal you blind if you let them."

Frequently, Max says, shoplifters slip in the front door of the store, grab whatever they can, and dash off down Hunts Point Avenue. "Nothing like that ever used to happen in the old days," he recalls. In recent months, the store has been burglarized twice. Like other business places in Hunts Point, Max's store is secured at night with a heavy barred gate that is pulled across the entrance. In addition, there are metal bars across the ceiling—intended to prevent thieves from breaking in through the roof of the one-story building. But, from all practical purposes, the bars might as well be made of kite string. "These guys [the burglars] just break them and come in anyway," Max says. "Both times they broke in here, they cleaned out the whole store. They didn't leave a thing." Even at that, Max considers himself somewhat lucky. "A fellow down the street who owns a dry-goods store has had five burglaries in the last seven months," he says.

The obvious question is: Why, in view of all the problems, do Max and his son keep the store in business? Part of the answer seems to lie in a sense of nostalgia—of loyalty to the Hunts Point that used to be. Until 1961, Max not only operated his business in Hunts Point; he also lived there, in a house at 754 Manida Street. The deterioration of the neighborhood persuaded him to move, so he became a permanent resident of the Concourse Plaza Hotel on the Grand Concourse in the West Bronx. But, reluctant to cut all ties with Hunts Point, he and his son decided to keep their store. "Listen, I remember this neighborhood when it was a wonderful place," Max says. "I remember when there were nanny goats right on the street corner here."

Sentimental memories of Hunts Point's yesterdays, to be

sure, are not the sole reason that Max and his son cling to the old store. They are, after all, merchants—not dabblers. They have found a way to make the store serve a useful purpose, even if it can no longer pay its own way as a retail outlet. In addition to operating the store, they carry on an active outside business—buying up the goods of other merchants who are closing down their shops because of bankruptcy or other reasons. Usually, in such cases, Max and his son are allowed to sell the purchased goods for brief periods from the other merchants' former premises. When the time comes for them to leave, they almost always have some merchandise left, and they need a place to store it for future sale. That's where the Hunts Point store comes in handy. "We use it as a warehouse," Max explains. "Actually, we keep it more for a warehouse than anything else." The convenience of having this storage space available makes up in part for the store's lack of profitability as a retail outlet.

But the fact is that it would be easy to find warehouse space available at far lower rent elsewhere than in a store on a busy thoroughfare—even one in a depressed area such as Hunts Point. Thus, in the final analysis, the attachment of Max and his son to their old neighborhood seems the most compelling reason for holding on to the store.

For every Max Vogel who has stayed in business in Hunts Point through its transformation into a ghetto, however, there have been many other merchants who have thrown up their hands in despair and fled. Throughout the neighborhood, abandoned stores and other business places—their doors and windows barred with wood against the onslaught of vandals—bear silent witness to the area's deterioration.

Next door to Max's store for many years was a meat market operated by a rotund, jolly butcher named Isadore Saidel. It was a family business. Not only Saidel's wife, Esther, but also his three children—Donald, Jean, and Rosalind—worked there at one time or another. The family, which lived a little more than a block away at 875 Irvine Street, was among the most admired in the neighborhood. Everybody in the family was intelligent, good-natured, generous, and responsible. The Saidels were Orthodox Jews who took their religion seriously. They worshiped regularly at a synagogue on Faile Street. They scrupulously kept the Sabbath. They observed the dietary laws. And, needless to say, they operated a kosher butcher shop.

As the Saidel children grew up, they gradually drifted away from Hunts Point. Rosalind married and moved to Long Beach, Long Island. Jean married and moved to Westchester County. Donald, after graduation from City College of New York, received a Ph.D. from the University of Kansas, married, became a psychologist, and moved to Baltimore. Their parents, meanwhile, stayed on in Hunts Point through the early and middle stages of the neighborhood's transformation. By 1961, however, it became clear that they would have to abandon the butcher shop. "There was no call for kosher meat there any more," says Isadore Saidel. "The people were almost all colored or Puerto Rican. They didn't want kosher meat." He wouldn't even consider converting the shop to a non-kosher operation, so he sold out. Later, he operated a kosher shop for several years in the Inwood section of Upper Manhattan, but is now retired and lives in the West Bronx. His former Hunts Point store was taken over by an auto-driving school specializing in helping Spanish-speaking residents get licenses.

While the Saidels' shop was flanked on the west by Max Vogel's store, it was flanked on the east by one of Hunts Point's most popular commercial establishments—a large luncheonette, candy, and stationery store, named simply "Joe's." For several generations of Hunts Pointers, the message "I'll meet you at Joe's" was the virtual Bronx equivalent of "I'll meet you under the clock at the Biltmore." Although it hardly appeared impressive—consisting merely of a soda fountain on one side, a row of booths on the other, some shelf space along the walls, and a small newsstand out front—Joe's was *the* place for Hunts Pointers to congregate.

Young children met there to buy bubble gum or trade baseball cards. Teen-agers met there for inexpensive dates, nursing milkshakes or sundaes for hours while they gossiped with friends. Young married women pushed their baby carriages there to meet friends for a cup of coffee. Middle-aged and elderly men and women met there to gossip. And some Hunts Pointers who made small bets with bookmakers met there many evenings to await the arrival of the bulldog editions of the next morning's newspapers, so they could check the sports scores and race results and the entries in the next day's races.

It was at Joe's that many Hunts Pointers caught their first glimpses of commercial television. When television sets first hit the market in large numbers after World War II, their cost was considered prohibitive by many Americans. To attract and hold customers, some business establishments—chiefly taverns, restaurants, and luncheonettes—installed coin-operated sets. In Hunts Point, the first such set was installed at Joe's. Customers took turns feeding quarters into the set, each of which bought fifteen minutes of viewing time. At the end of the fifteen minutes, the screen would go dark until another quarter was inserted. Invariably, a crucial point in the show would be missed while several customers tried to out-fumble each other to avoid inserting the quarter that would relight the screen.

One night, Joe's was packed with Hunts Pointers anxious to see a local hero on the screen. The hero was a native son named Stan Starkman, better known by the nickname Stitch. For several years, Stitch had been known as one of the best playground basketball players in New York City. If put on any outdoor basketball court for a pickup game, he was a sensation—tossing in seemingly impossible shots from all over the place. But for some reason, he was never able to convert his talent to maximum use on an organized team. Clair Bee, the veteran coach at Long Island University, tried for three years to mold Stitch's undisciplined style into a pattern that would make him a college star. He failed miserably. But now, incredibly, Stitch had been signed to a contract with a New York professional team named the Gothams. And the Gothams' games were occasionally carried on television. The night of Stitch's first appearance with the team, the crowd surrounding the television set at Joe's was perhaps the largest ever to fill the luncheonette. Impatiently, the Hunts Pointers waited for their hero's appearance. The first quarter dragged by, then the second, and the third. Stitch had yet to enter the game. Finally, late in the fourth quarter, the sportscaster announced: "Stan Starkman, just signed by the Gothams, is taking off his jacket and getting ready to come into the game."

The words had no sooner been uttered than the image on the screen began to fade. Then it went black. "Who's got a quarter?" someone asked. Hands frantically plunged into pockets, but nobody could come up with a quarter. There were nickels, dimes, pennies, folding money—but no quarters. Someone pushed his way through the crowd to the cash register, where he hurriedly exchanged a dollar bill for four quarters. A path was cleared, so he could run to the TV set. When he inserted the quarter, the sportscaster's voice could be heard, saying: "Now, Stan Starkman is returning to the bench."

During the brief period in which the screen had been black, Stitch had gotten his hands on the ball and taken one of his patented playground shots—a sweeping hook shot off the backboard from near the right sideline. The shot had plunked from the board straight through the net. Although he had scored two points, the shot had not endeared Stitch to the Gothams' coach. He thought it looked too much like a playground "heave"—in short, too unprofessional for a team such as the Gothams—so he had immediately yanked Stitch from the game. For the remainder of the last quarter, Stitch rode the bench. His career on the Gothams ended a short time later without his appearance in another televised game. His fans at Joe's—deprived of their big chance to view him on the screen—thereafter had to content themselves with watching him back on the playgrounds. Today, he is a New York City policeman and no longer lives in Hunts Point, but can occasionally still be seen flipping in one-handers on the asphalt outdoor courts of the city.

Joe's, like the Saidels' butcher shop and many other enterprises in Hunts Point, was for years a family business. The owner, Joe Schein, tended the store with his wife and their three sons—Harold, Gerald, and Martin. In addition, the place provided part-time employment to a succession of Hunts Point's young men who were working their way through college. Among them were two friends of Harold Schein, Merton (Mertie) Berlinger and Leonard (Lenny) Schwartz, both students at City College of New York. Mertie was one of the most industrious workers ever employed at Joe's, constantly buzzing around the place on one mission or another—waiting on customers in the booths, jerking sodas, making ice-cream cones. Lenny was hardly such a dynamo. He did what was demanded of him, but little more. Yet for the longest time, when they compared notes Mertie would discover to his amazement that Lenny was taking home far more money in tips than he was. How could that be? It nearly drove Mertie to distraction. Finally, he got his answer. One day, he noticed that Lenny—while assiduously avoiding all other tasks—was voluntarily wiping off the tables in the booths where Mertie had waited on customers. In the process, he was pocketing the tips. Lenny thought it was a riot that he'd been getting away with the stunt for months, but Mertie almost committed mayhem on him. An amicable settlement was reached and the two, amazingly, remained close friends.

When Hunts Point began undergoing its deterioration, business at Joe's suffered less than at many other establishments in the neighborhood. The new Puerto Rican and Negro residents, while they found no need to patronize kosher butcher shops and certain other local businesses, did stop in at Joe's. And, for a time, many of the store's old customers remained in the neighborhood. So the Schein family held on to the store. With the passage of time, however, increasing numbers of old-time Hunts Pointers moved away, and the new residents failed to take up the slack. The newcomers, while they might stop occasionally at Joe's, did not have enough money to come there as often as the old-timers had. Business dropped off, and prospects were that it would drop even further in the future. In addition, Joe's sons were now grown, married, and pursuing careers. There would be nobody in the family to take over the business when Joe retired. So there seemed little reason for him to hold on any longer to a business that figured to go nowhere but downhill in the coming years. Joe ultimately sold the store and moved to Florida.

Today, the store is still there and it is still called Joe's. At lunchtime, it still does a fairly substantial business under its new owners. And throughout the day, there is a relatively steady flow of customers. But the store is not the Joe's of old by any means. No longer is it one of Hunts Point's favorite hangouts—a place to meet friends or while away the hours. Nowadays, its customers do not tarry there; they make their purchases, gulp down their sandwiches or coffee, and are on their way in a matter of minutes. In short, it is just another luncheonette.

About a mile east of Joe's, at the corner of Randall Avenue and Hunts Point Avenue, is a Shell Oil Company outlet called the Randall Service Station. Its manager is a tall, handsome native Hunts Pointer named Bob Rice. "My father's owned the station for thirty-six years," Bob says. "I've been around Hunts Point most of my life. I was born in Hunts Point Hospital—on June 19, 1947. We lived for many years on Casanova Street, first at 663, then at 665, and later at 667. When I was a kid, I went to school at St. Athanasius [a parochial school operated by the local Catholic church]. We live upstate now, in Mt. Kisco, but we've held on to the station, so I've been here all through the changing of the neighborhood."

Although Hunts Point was already beginning to deteriorate while he was a child, Bob can recall some of its better days. "When I was a kid, it was still a pretty good neighborhood," he says. "The private houses and apartment buildings were in good condition. There wasn't all this crime. People weren't afraid to be on the streets. I can remember going by myself down to the Tiffany Street dock, on the East River, and going swimming. Now, a kid's not safe on the streets alone."

Because of the crime and depressed conditions in the neighborhood, business at the service station has been hurt. To reduce the possibility of losses from thefts, the station keeps only a limited stock of auto parts—making it necessary to put in frequent calls to suppliers as particular items are needed. Hardly a week goes by without the station being victimized in one way or another by Hunts Point's criminal element.

"There's a trucking company that parks its trucks on our back lot at night," Bob says. "There are six trucks. In the last week or two, the batteries have been stolen—one at a time— out of four of them."

Asked what he thought could be done to reduce crime in Hunts Point, he replies: "The main thing is to get rid of the junkies." But how? "I'm not sure, but I'll tell you one idea that worked in a small area around here. Up on Hunts Point

Avenue, between Garrison Avenue and Lafayette Avenue, a bunch of buildings were refurbished not long ago. After the repairs were made, the people living there got together and put up a sign that said: 'Junkies, stay out of here. We don't want you.' And then, by God, they stuck together and made sure the junkies did stay out. Of course, that was a small area, as I said, and the junkies kept operating nearby. I don't know whether an idea like that would be practical for the whole neighborhood, but if you could somehow get all the decent people to pull together it might work." The apparent fly in such an ointment is that nobody has yet been able to mobilize the decent residents throughout Hunts Point to co-operate on anything.

The Randall Service Station is a short distance from the entrance to the Hunts Point Market. And from his vantage point at the station, Bob says he can see one of the few thriving businesses still extant in Hunts Point. "Just look out there," he says, gesturing in the direction of the market entrance. "There must be twenty whores out there right now. They're out there all the time, and they're doing a land-office business. We call them the neighborhood's school-crossing guards. They're out there, rain or shine, just like crossing guards. What really gets me is that police cars go by them all the time and the cops never do anything about them."

The market itself is the site of the bulk of the highly profitable businesses currently operating in Hunts Point. Within its 126 acres, there are 4,000 to 4,500 persons at work during peak periods. But most of them, as previously pointed out, are not Hunts Pointers. They are persons who have been employed in the produce business for perhaps twenty-five or thirty-five years and formerly worked in the old Washington Street Market in Lower Manhattan.

The market was built by the city government at a cost of $35 million. The city, in turn, rents space to private firms—

chiefly wholesale produce merchants and large supermarket chains. In addition, the city collects tolls from all vehicles entering the market. By train and by truck, the market receives produce originally shipped from virtually all of the fifty states and from numerous foreign countries. Most goods pass through the market and are on retail shelves within twenty-four hours of receipt. Often, the produce does not even enter the wholesaler's rented premises. A freight car pulls up to a railroad siding adjacent to the wholesaler's space. He then allows retailers to inspect the merchandise inside the car, place their orders, and then back their trucks up to the freight car and receive their goods. Officials estimate that 23 million persons in the New York region buy produce handled by the market.

Although the market is open around the clock, the bulk of its work is done at night in order to get the produce on retail shelves in time for early-morning shoppers. It is a colorful place, filled with merchandise both ordinary and exotic, and with an assortment of individualists who take great delight in haggling over prices. "Five dollars a box for this crap?" asks one retailer, pointing to a crate of melons. "You gotta be kiddin' me." A wholesaler laughs. "You never change, Charlie," he says. "If I said a dollar a box, you'd still be pissin' and moanin'." Charlie affects an injured air. "Come on, charge me a little less," he argues. "Let me make a livin'." They eventually agree on four and a half dollars a box. Charlie looks ecstatic; he has won again.

As previously discussed, the market is plagued by crime. William Neenan, an inspector for the City Department of Ports and Terminals (which operates the market), says: "Our biggest problem in the market is security. Anyone found inside the market without proper credentials is subject to arrest for unlawful entry, but a lot of thieves get inside anyway. There's a great deal of pilfering. We're trying to cope with it, but it's very difficult. There are so many narcotics addicts around here, who will do anything for money, that we just can't keep up with them all."

Adjacent to the market, construction is underway at this writing on various other projects that will eventually bring additional business establishments to the area. Plans call for the Fulton Street fish market, the city's wholesale meat market, and the wholesale flower market to be relocated there. Unlike the produce market, these markets are being built with private funds.

Under other circumstances, these new business places might have been welcomed by residents of Hunts Point. But the problem is that, like the produce market, they are expected to provide few jobs for Hunts Point residents and few benefits for the local business community. They are expected to bring with them most of their workers now employed in other parts of the city. And there is little hope that they will do any more than the produce market did to revitalize the depressed business conditions in Hunts Point, since they will be dealing chiefly with firms from outside the neighborhood.

Thus, many Hunts Pointers regard construction of the new market sites as still another example of the exploitation of the neighborhood by outside forces—with the concurrence of the city government, which approved the relocation plans. As one Hunts Point resident, Mrs. Olivia White, puts it: "All these places—these markets—don't contribute a damn thing to this neighborhood. They ain't givin' us nothin'. All they're doin' is takin', takin', takin'. We got enough people takin' from us already. We don't need no more!"

15

We have seen how Hunts Point used to be and how it is now. We have seen the sort of people who used to live there and the sort who live there now. We have seen how a relaxed, relatively comfortable way of life has been replaced by a helter-skelter existence marked by deprivation and terror. But four major questions remain to be discussed. First, why did the deterioration of Hunts Point take place in such a short time, compared with the more gradual eroding of other neighborhoods that became ghettos? Second, what could have been done to prevent such deterioration? Third, what can be done, if anything, to save Hunts Point? Fourth, what are the national implications of the Hunts Point story, and what lessons does this story provide for other communities throughout the country?

The reasons for the rapid deterioration of Hunts Point were many and complex. Some were geographic, some economic, some determined by migration patterns of poor families entering New York City from Puerto Rico and elsewhere. As background, it is instructive to examine briefly the history of slum life elsewhere in New York City.

Harlem, the New York slum perhaps most easily identifiable by out-of-towners, had been occupied chiefly by Negroes for decades before it deteriorated into a ghetto. At one time,

Harlem had been occupied by whites—many of them rather well-to-do whites. But, as the migration of Negroes from the South to northern cities increased the black population of New York City, Harlem gradually was taken over by Negroes. It was in good condition when they arrived and remained that way for years. Although there were many poor Negroes in Harlem from the start, there were also sizable numbers of middle-class and wealthy blacks. The more affluent residents by and large took excellent care of their homes and encouraged their poorer neighbors to do likewise. Thus, while Harlem became a basically Negro enclave in a relatively short period, it did not become a slum until much later.

There was a great sense of community pride in Harlem. It had its own culture, its own writers, its own artists, its own musicians, its own newspaper (the *Amsterdam News*), its own radio stations, its own political organizations, its own religious figures, its own heroes. When the United States entered World War I, Harlem even contributed its own military unit—an all-Negro outfit called the 369th Infantry Regiment. The 369th was the first unit of the Allied armies to reach the Rhine. It served longer under fire (191 days) than any other regiment in the American Expeditionary Force, never yielded a single prisoner, never surrendered a foot of ground, and suffered higher casualties than perhaps any other outfit. Forty percent of its men were either killed or wounded.

By 1940, there were more than 458,000 Negroes in New York City, and most of them lived in Harlem. The federal census that year disclosed that Harlem contained more Negroes to the square mile than any other spot on earth. Conditions were beginning to deteriorate by that time, as the housing became more crowded and some of the wealthier blacks left Harlem for other neighborhoods in New York and its suburbs. Still, there were enough Negroes with money so that

Harlem had its own "horsy set" that rode regularly in Central Park.

By 1943, however, there was sufficient discontent with conditions in Harlem that bloody anti-white rioting erupted. The rioting was attributed to a variety of grievances—including racial discrimination, overcrowding, lack of facilities, rent- and price-gouging, and resentment of civilian violence directed against Negroes serving in the armed forces during that World War II year. From that time on, conditions in Harlem continued to deteriorate as ever larger numbers of poor Negroes moved in and more fortunate Negroes left.

When immigrants from Puerto Rico and other spots in Latin America began their mass migration to New York, resulting chiefly from depressed economic conditions at home, it was natural for them to seek places to live at the lowest possible rents. At first, some of them moved into Harlem. But the housing there was so crowded that it could accommodate only limited numbers of new residents. Thus, the Latins sought housing nearby—in what has come to be called East Harlem or Spanish Harlem. That area, on the Upper East Side of Manhattan, gradually became a slum, whose depressed conditions paralleled—and in some cases were even worse than—those in black Harlem.

As the migration of Puerto Ricans, other Latins, and Negroes continued, the housing in Harlem and East Harlem surpassed the bursting point. There was simply no more room there for the immigrants, so they began moving across the Harlem River into the South Bronx. The old middle-class white residents of the South Bronx, in what has become a classic pattern, kept moving farther north and east to avoid what they considered the horrors of living among the darker-skinned newcomers. In short order, Hunts Point was surrounded by areas occupied chiefly by Negroes and Puerto Ricans. On the south were mainly Puerto Ricans who had been unable to find housing in East Harlem. On the west were mainly Negroes who had settled in a black colony around Prospect Avenue when they had been unable to find housing in Harlem.

What made Hunts Point different from other sections occupied by whites who felt threatened by the "invasion" of their neighborhoods was that it was, in effect, the end of the line. It was bordered on two sides by water—the Bronx River and the East River. On the other two sides were the Puerto Ricans and Negroes the whites wanted to avoid. Whereas whites in other neighborhoods confronted by the "encroachment" of blacks and Latins could gradually move farther and farther away from the advancing newcomers, there was no room for Hunts Pointers to maneuver in this fashion. They were hemmed in by the rivers on two sides. They were faced with two alternatives—stay where they were and coexist with the newcomers, or move completely out of the neighborhood. Most chose to flee.

Thus, Hunts Point was thrown open in a very short period to all the worst horrors characterized by the term "changing neighborhood." The block-busters moved in with a vengeance, frightening home-owners into panic sales. Prices paid by these leeches to the departing owners were minimal, but those they charged to newcomers were inflated. Tenants in two-family and three-family houses and in apartment houses fled concurrently with the home-owners. Block after block saw its population change from white to black and Latin. The wave of immigrants spread swiftly toward the rivers. (It was because the neighborhood surrounding P.S. 48 was closer to the East River than were other sections of Hunts Point that the migration reached it last. That is why this neighborhood is today considered in slightly better condition than other sections.)

It is perhaps unfair to conclude that, merely because the white middle-class residents of a neighborhood are replaced by poor blacks and Puerto Ricans, the neighborhood will

[182]

necessarily deteriorate. There certainly have been occasions when such has not been the case. But the fact, unfortunately, is that such cases are the exception rather than the rule. Far more often, as in the case of Hunts Point, occupation by poor Negroes and Latin-Americans leads quickly to neighborhood decay. (It should be added that the newcomers' ethnic backgrounds are probably incidental. If they were poor whites, the deterioration might well be identical. But in most major cities—and particularly in New York—there is no practical way to test this theory because the number of desperately poor whites does not approach the number of destitute Negroes or Puerto Ricans.)

What were the reasons for the deterioration in Hunts Point? First, the number of incoming Negroes and Puerto Ricans far exceeded the number of outgoing whites. Thus, the existing housing soon was virtually bursting at the seams. Three, four, and even five persons were occupying rooms designed for one. Such overcrowding invariably produced intolerable conditions, in which the housing facilities were bound to suffer. Second, most of the new residents were tenants, rather than property-owners. Moreover, many of them were virtual transients—constantly moving from one building to another. Such residents had less incentive to care for their dwellings than had prior occupants who had either owned their own homes or rented apartments on a long-term basis. Third, the absentee landlords who owned many Hunts Point buildings stopped providing proper maintenance. Some said they could not make enough money on the buildings to afford the maintenance costs, since tenants frequently defaulted on their rents or fell months behind. Others clearly were determined to milk the buildings for all they were worth, collecting the highest rents possible and providing minimum services. Fourth, the Negroes and Puerto Ricans who moved into Hunts Point were not only poor—they were the poorest of the poor. By and large, they were the most recent newcomers to the city. Many of the jobs they sought had already been snapped up by Negroes and Puerto Ricans who had come earlier to New York. And even those who found work were compelled to accept the bare minimum wages. Thus, many of the new Hunts Pointers were forced onto the welfare rolls. Others turned to crime, which begat still further deterioration of the neighborhood. The depressed conditions bred despair that led many to seek escape in any fashion they could find—narcotics, alcohol, whatever. This, in turn, led to still further crime. Fifth, the increasingly desperate plight of the residents placed heavy burdens on the forces of government. More people—and poorer people— required more schoolrooms, more police and fire protection, more frequent garbage collection, greater health and social services, and the like. But the city government was either unable or unwilling to provide these services; it was in serious financial trouble and saw its chief priorities elsewhere than Hunts Point. In many cases, the new Hunts Pointers found that not only were they not getting the increased services they needed; they were not even getting the services that their more affluent predecessors had received.

All of these factors, and others, were responsible for Hunts Point's rapid deterioration. One element that cannot be overlooked is the frustration and hostility engendered by the deterioration itself. People who feel victimized by events beyond their control tend to lash out at the closest available targets, even if the venting of their wrath hurts them as well as their real or imagined enemies. Thus, a slum-dweller who is angry at his landlord may deliberately break the plumbing fixtures in his own apartment. The fact that he is depriving himself of the facilities somehow seems secondary to the fact that he is "getting even" with the landlord. Or, as a means of showing his hostility toward the city government, someone may dump garbage out his window onto the street. The fact that it is he, rather than city officials, who will have to walk through that garbage or fend off the rats it may attract also seems secondary.

By such means did the deterioration of Hunts Point proceed. It was accelerated further by the continuing migration of Negroes and Puerto Ricans into the area. Congressman Herman Badillo estimates that, between 1960 and 1970, more than 500,000 blacks and Puerto Ricans entered New York City, and an approximately equal number of whites left. Many of those new Puerto Ricans and blacks moved into Hunts Point. The most recent estimate is that there are about 84,000 Puerto Ricans in Hunts Point, 55,000 Negroes, and 20,000 classified as "others." (The "others" include whites, Orientals, and some Latin-Americans who came from places other than Puerto Rico.) When one considers that the population of the area was composed chiefly of white middle-class residents two decades ago, the speed with which the neighborhood changed complexion becomes apparent.

Could the deterioration of Hunts Point have been prevented? And, if so, how?

Given the conditions that prevailed, it may well be that some deterioration was inevitable. But it also seems clear that this deterioration could have been limited—kept within bounds that would have prevented Hunts Point from sinking to its current depths. For one thing, many of the white middle-class residents who had lived in Hunts Point for years— even generations—could have resisted the pressures to panic and flee. Large numbers of the home-owners who deserted Hunts Point did so because they believed the old bugaboo that property values would plummet once Negroes and Puerto Ricans moved into the neighborhood. But experience elsewhere has shown that the mere entry of minority groups does not necessarily reduce property values. In fact, in some cases where true integration has taken place, property values actually have risen. Had large numbers of whites remained in Hunts Point and coexisted with Negroes and Puerto Ricans (obviously smaller numbers of Negroes and Puerto Ricans than ultimately occupied the area when the whites left), there is reason to believe that property values would at least have remained stable.

If these whites had stayed and the incoming Negroes and Puerto Ricans had been integrated into the neighborhood, there is every reason to believe that the deterioration would have been sharply curbed. The sheer size of Hunts Point's population would have been limited. The number of poor residents would likewise have been kept reasonably low. There would have been far fewer absentee landlords. The strain on municipal services would have been kept within manageable bounds. It is reasonable to assume that narcotics addiction and other crime would have been contained at far lower levels than eventually resulted.

There was much that government could have done to prevent Hunts Point's decay. The city government, for example, could have enforced the laws limiting the number of persons who may occupy certain dwellings. Instead, the city ignored these laws—permitting the overcrowding that played a large role in Hunts Point's deterioration. (It may be argued that the people who crowded into Hunts Point needed *some* place to stay and that the city couldn't very well force them out on the streets. But that is begging the question. The city could have, and should have, seen to it that these people had decent places to live without jamming into tight quarters in such numbers that they violated the law.)

The city, state, and federal governments could have pooled their efforts to provide decent low-cost housing in Hunts Point. Throughout New York City, including most slum areas, there are relatively new housing projects for low-income tenants. While it is true that conditions in some of these projects are far from ideal, they are certainly far better than in the tenements in Hunts Point. Such projects abound

[186]

in the areas near Hunts Point. Yet, there is not a single project within Hunts Point itself.

Private enterprise deserves its share of the blame for refusing to put up more than token amounts of money to build non-public housing in the area. While the reluctance of private developers to invest in a decaying neighborhood is perhaps understandable, it hardly accords with the frequent claims of big businessmen that they are taking meaningful steps to revitalize the slums. Moreover, the excuses given by developers for refusing to invest in Hunts Point—such as the contention that any buildings they construct there will inevitably be torn apart by tenants and outsiders—have not been supported by events. In the few cases in which private investors have built decent new apartment houses in Hunts Point recently, the buildings have remained in excellent condition and enjoyed relatively full occupancy. One such building, an elevator apartment house on Faile Street at its intersection with Hunts Point Avenue, has become the showplace of the neighborhood. It is immaculate, free from vandalism, and provides its tenants tight security. There is no apparent reason why other new buildings could not be equally successful if investors were willing to construct them.

Considering the monumental law-enforcement problems that developed in Hunts Point, it is perhaps unfair to criticize the police. In the main, they seem to have been trying to make the best of an extremely difficult situation. But, at the same time, at least some of the complaints by citizens about police indifference appear justified. Some officers in the 41st Precinct do seem so inured to Hunts Point's crime epidemic that they ignore all but the most serious offenses. In addition, it is clear that the manpower assigned to the precinct is woefully inadequate. Had the city government and the top officials of the police department moved early in the game to beef up manpower in the precinct, and had policemen in the precinct dealt more aggressively with the burgeoning criminal element at the outset of Hunts Point's deterioration, the crime problem might well have been kept within more reasonable bounds.

The lack of enforcement was particularly acute in relation to narcotics dealers and addicts. Almost any officer in the 41st Precinct can take a walking tour of the neighborhood and, within a couple of hours, spot several hundred addicts. He knows these people are addicts, thieves, and in some cases, narcotics-sellers. Yet, they are still on the streets. Of course, a policeman's mere suspicion or even knowledge that a person is addicted is not sufficient to sustain an arrest. But every addict needs at least several fixes a day. Thus, he is forced to violate the law daily by possessing narcotics. At least every few days, he usually must violate another law by buying drugs. And, in the ordinary course of events, he must steal, pimp, or engage in some other form of crime in order to get the money he needs to buy narcotics. Critics of police in the 41st Precinct argue that intensive surveillance of junkies would inevitably lead to their arrests, since they couldn't go about their usual activities for more than a half-day without violating one law or another.

Policemen reply that they haven't had the manpower to carry out such surveillance on a large-scale basis. They contend that they are often compelled by their limited manpower and resources to ignore the common street peddler or user of narcotics in order to go after the important wholesalers. They point out, for example, that one of the largest narcotics raids in American history took place in Hunts Point—the seizure of eighty-five pounds of heroin worth an estimated $20 million in the basement of an apartment house at 1171 Bryant Avenue. This raid was the culmination of the case that formed the basis for the book and movie entitled *The French Connection*. But the fact is that the raid was not pulled by officers of the 41st Precinct; it was carried out by federal agents and detectives from the police department's citywide anti-narcotics force. In fact, officers from the 41st Precinct unwittingly almost ruined the investigation. Several times, unaware of the fact that federal agents and detectives were staked out in the Bryant Avenue building, uniformed officers showed up to investigate reports that mysterious men (those on stakeout) were lurking in the building. Their arrival narrowly missed tipping off the suspects.

Although some of the excuses given by officers of the 41st Precinct seem reasonable, it nonetheless appears evident that far more could have been done to curb the narcotics traffic in Hunts Point ever since the beginning of the neighborhood's deterioration. The failure to mount an effective anti-narcotics campaign has created immeasurable problems—not only in the misery of the addicts, but also in the crimes they have committed and in the general decay that has resulted in the neighborhood.

Similarly, in assessing what could have been done to limit Hunts Point's deterioration, it is clear that virtually every city agency could have done far more. The sanitation department could have prevented, or at least curbed, the massive accumulation of garbage and debris by throwing additional manpower and equipment into a continuing cleanup campaign. Instead, the department cut back on service in Hunts Point—in effect throwing up its hands and pronouncing the problem insoluble. City building and health inspectors could have cracked down on landlords who allowed tenants to live in filth and misery in substandard buildings. Instead, many of them turned their backs and permitted the landlords to get away with providing ever-diminishing services. In the end, when the buildings were no longer profitable, large numbers of them were simply abandoned by the landlords and taken over by the city. At that point, the city could have launched a campaign to rehabilitate them. Instead, it declared many of them unfit for human habitation and yet allowed tenants to continue living there. City officials argued that this was the humane thing to do, since they didn't want to put the tenants out on the streets, but there was nothing to prevent them from making at least emergency repairs while the residents remained in the buildings. Still, they did not.

To take Hunts Point children off the streets and channel their energies away from narcotics and crime into wholesome activities, the city could have provided the neighborhood with new recreation facilities. Many parents pleaded for the establishment of a community center for the area's young people. City officials not only turned down the request; they also stood by and watched as existing outdoor recreation facilities, such as small parks and playgrounds, were allowed to deteriorate because of inadequate supervision.

City officials also turned aside, for long periods, appeals by parents, teachers, and school administrators that new and larger schools were urgently needed in Hunts Point. The officials claimed they didn't have the money to build such schools. Hunts Point children would just have to make do with the ancient, dilapidated schools already in existence. Under heavy pressure, the city ultimately did agree to build another elementary school near P.S. 48 in the next few years. But construction has not yet started, and there is no assurance when it will. Meanwhile, the city has somehow found the funds to build not one school but a so-called educational park—containing two primary schools, two intermediate schools (grades five through eight), a senior high, gymnasiums, two swimming pools, a 1,200-seat auditorium, a 400-seat little theater, athletic fields, and a planetarium—in the more affluent Co-op City housing development in the northeast Bronx. Such an educational park might have been ideal for Hunts Point, where an estimated 27,000 students are crowded into sixteen primary, intermediate, and junior high schools—most of them more than forty years old—and where there is not a single high school. Yet there is no indication that the city even considered placing that sort of facility in Hunts Point. Hunts Pointers considered themselves lucky to win the promise of eventual construction of an additional elementary school.

To halt the rise of unemployment in Hunts Point—which is three times the national average—the city could have worked with private enterprise in a campaign to lure new businesses to the area and prevent existing businesses from leaving. The city did virtually nothing to halt the outflow of businesses, and its major attempt to bring new business in— the construction of the Hunts Point Market—provided few jobs for local residents. As previously discussed, the produce merchants who moved into the market brought with them long-established staffs and thus had little need for new employees from Hunts Point. The city has a department whose chief function is to attract new industry and prevent existing businesses from leaving New York. In Hunts Point, there is a vast pool of potential workers—particularly the kind of unskilled laborers who are needed for factory work. There is vacant land zoned for industrial use. There are even vacant factory buildings that could be converted to new uses by incoming industries. Yet, neither city officials nor businessmen have taken advantage of these conditions. They have allowed industry to flee Hunts Point without being replaced, and thus made it inevitable that unemployment in the area would increase at a dizzying pace. The city, amid a fanfare of publicity, did make one feeble effort to improve the business climate in Hunts Point—but it fell on its face.

This effort was part of a project known as Operation Main Street, which was sponsored by the City Economic Development Administration. The idea was to spruce up fifteen neighborhood shopping areas throughout the city, where business had dropped substantially because of urban decay, and thus try to lure customers back to the stores. The Economic Development Administration—in cooperation with such other city agencies as the police, sanitation, traffic, and highway departments—was supposed to try to provide the shopping areas with better protection, cleaner streets, better parking facilities, and other conditions that would prove attractive to customers. Among the fifteen areas chosen for the project was a section of Hunts Point on Southern Boulevard, between Westchester Avenue and 163rd Street. The problem was that there was more fanfare than action. Hunts Point shoppers never saw any substantial improvement in conditions. And, as one merchant put it, "They [city officials] aren't putting any real money into this thing. It's mostly a public-relations program." In an area with Hunts Point's problems, a mere public-relations program won't cut it. Besides, even if the project had been successful, it would have affected only about two blocks—hardly making a dent in the neighborhood's decay.

It is impossible to try to assess what could have been done to prevent Hunts Point's deterioration without, in the final analysis, placing a heavy share of responsibility on the new residents who moved into the area. True, they were saddled with heavy burdens. True, many of them moved in after the decay had begun and were seemingly powerless to turn back the clock. True, many of them had so much trouble learning merely to survive that they had little time or energy for civic-betterment campaigns.

Still, it was many of these very people who tossed garbage out their windows to decay and stink up their own neighborhood. It was many of these very people who vandalized the buildings in which they lived, who urinated and defecated in the hallways. It was many of these very people who allowed their children to roam the streets until all hours of the night. And it was many of these very people who turned to narcotics and thievery. In Hunts Point, it is sometimes difficult to separate the violators from the violated. In many cases, the two categories overlap.

But it cannot be left unsaid that if many of these new residents had shown more responsibility—if they had taken more pride in their homes and their behavior—much of Hunts Point's deterioration might have been averted. It is one thing to understand the reasons for their irresponsibility; it is quite another thing to ignore it.

16

If the past is indeed prologue, the question becomes what will happen to Hunts Point now. Can it be saved? And, if so, how?

The answer to the question about the possibility of its salvation seems to be not only that it can be saved but that it must be saved. If the richest, most industrialized, most ingenious nation on earth cannot reclaim a neighborhood that has rotted within two decades, it might just as well commit suicide by detonating its nuclear arsenal. It has become a cliché to compare the country's fantastic successes in exploring outer space with its failures on other fronts. But cliché or not, any nation with the capacity to place men on the moon and to send spacecraft to examine Mars must *per se* have the capacity to save a neighborhood such as Hunts Point from dying.

On the question of how to go about it, the first hurdle to be cleared is mustering the will to do the job. There is no getting around the fact that it will cost substantial, even enormous, amounts of money. But the money is there if the people of Hunts Point, New Yorkers generally, and other Americans have the will to spend it for the tasks at hand. Some perspective is needed on the priorities of our national spending programs. President Nixon, for example, has proposed appropriating $11 billion for a campaign to save the decaying cities—not one urban neighborhood such as Hunts Point, not one city, but $11 billion for all of the nation's cities. Now, $11 billion is hardly a trifling amount, but it seems a mere pittance when stacked up against the needs of Hunts Point and other urban ghettos. It also seems a pittance when compared with some other federal spending programs. To wit, under a federal law called the National Defense Highway Act, the government launched a massive road-building campaign whose ostensible purpose was to provide the armed forces with the capacity to send weapons and other supplies to strategic parts of the country in case of a military emergency. In this age of nuclear missiles and super-sonic aircraft, many Americans were never convinced that such a highway system was necessary for military prepared-ness. Yet the government spent $60 billion on the defense highways—almost six times the amount President Nixon proposes to spend on saving the cities. Moreover, the gov-ernment has been spending upwards of $80 billion a year on national defense and more than $25 billion a year in military support for Southeast Asia. It would seem that a country that spent such amounts annually on defense against its foreign enemies could afford more than $11 billion for a long-range program to combat such home-front enemies as poverty, crime, and disease in the urban ghettos.

Thus, the question is how can the people of Hunts Point and other slum areas persuade both the government and pri-vate members of the so-called Establishment to create a new set of priorities that will truly seek to overcome the problems of the cities—rather than merely to apply makeshift, tem-porary remedies. One suggestion, made only partially with tongue in cheek, was put forward by a former mayor of Minneapolis, Arthur Natfalin. He proposed that the cities simply surrender and tell the federal government: "We've

lost the war. Now, rebuild us like Germany and Japan."
Natfalin's sarcasm aside, the situation may yet come to
that.

But even for such a massive rebuilding campaign to begin,
there must be a drastic rethinking of the relation of major
cities to the nation at large. It is hardly a secret that, although the bulk of the nation's population and problems lie
in the cities, both Congress and most state legislatures are
dominated by representatives of rural interests.

The people holding the purse strings of federal and state
governments are essentially anti-urban. It has been that way
ever since the United States was born. Thomas Jefferson
summarized the anti-urban position two centuries ago, and
his philosophy has been adopted by countless followers over
the years. "I think our governments will remain virtuous for
centuries as long as they are chiefly agricultural," Jefferson
said. "When they get piled upon one another in large cities,
as in Europe, they will become as corrupt as in Europe."

Well, the people and governments have gotten piled upon
one another in places such as Hunts Point, and they have,
perhaps, become corrupt. But the "virtuousness" of their
rural brethren is certainly open to question as well. If it is
virtuous for a Congress dominated by rural Southerners to
deny meaningful aid to dying cities while appropriating bil-
lions of dollars for artificial farm-price supports and military
bases or near-bankrupt defense contractors in their home
states, then we need a new definition of virtue.

As has been seen, the indifference to Hunts Point's problems does not lie solely at the federal and state levels. Within
the city government itself, where there presumably is an appreciation of the need for urban revitalization, Hunts Point
has been treated as a forgotten area. So there must be a
reordering of priorities in the city government, as well as the
state and federal governments, if Hunts Point is to be saved.
But how can this reordering of priorities be brought about?

The first step must be the acquisition of a measure of political clout by Hunts Pointers. One of the chief drawbacks during the period of Hunts Point's deterioration has been the almost total absence of political mobilization within the neighborhood. Other ghettos in New York City, such as Harlem and Bedford-Stuyvesant, have received far more attention than Hunts Point because they have been represented by powerful political organizations. For all his purported faults, former Congressman Adam Clayton Powell saw to it for years that his Harlem constituents' interests were protected not only on Capitol Hill but at all levels of government. Congresswoman Shirley Chisholm has fulfilled a similar role for the residents of Bedford-Stuyvesant and other nearby slums. But there has been no Adam Powell or Shirley Chisholm for Hunts Point. Congressman James Scheuer, who represents most of Hunts Point, seems to be a sincere, dedicated politician who is doing his best for his constituents. But his district includes many other areas of the Bronx outside Hunts Point. Beyond that, he does not appear to have the charisma to mobilize Hunts Pointers into an effective political bloc. Furthermore, he is neither black nor Puerto Rican, but a white, Jewish lawyer—so many Hunts Pointers find it difficult to identify with him. Congressman Herman Badillo, a Puerto Rican who does have an abundance of charisma, is the type of politician around whom many Hunts Pointers might rally. The problem has been that his congressional district has included only a small sliver of Hunts Point and has also included other sections of not only the Bronx but also Manhattan and Queens. That problem has been compounded by a 1972 reapportionment of congressional districts that threatens to work to the further detriment of Hunts Pointers.

Another major reason for the absence of political power within Hunts Point has been the very makeup of its citizenry. The fact that more than half of present-day Hunts Pointers are Puerto Ricans—many of whom don't speak more than a smattering of English—is particularly significant. All ghetto residents experience trouble in achieving political power. But Latin-Americans, especially Puerto Ricans, experience perhaps more trouble than any others.

For one thing, they have the language barrier working against them. They often cannot adequately communicate their views to their elected representatives. Many of them not only are unable to read the English-language newspapers or understand the newscasts that might put them in closer touch with the world around them—they do not even read the Spanish-language newspapers that are available in New York and certain other American cities. Moreover, they do not have a tradition of political activism on which to draw.

In predominantly Negro ghettos, such as Harlem, there has been effective political action for decades. This action was accelerated by the civil rights revolution of the 1950's and 1960's. But there has been no comparable movement in areas such as Hunts Point. It is precisely such a movement that is necessary if Hunts Pointers are to mobilize politically to save their community.

The urgency of such political action was outlined recently in a 192-page report on New York's Puerto Ricans written by a Fordham University sociologist, the Reverend Joseph P. Fitzpatrick. Pointing out that the Puerto Ricans in the city had thus far failed to achieve "community solidarity," Father Fitzpatrick attributed the problem largely to the fact that they did not truly consider New York their home. "The proximity of the island [Puerto Rico] and the ease of return seem to prompt the Puerto Ricans to find in the island the sense of strength, support, and identity that former immigrants found in the clusters of their own kind in the immigrant communities of American cities," he wrote. "There is a great deal of truth in the comment that this is not a Puerto Rican migration but a process of Puerto Rican commuting." Still, although many Puerto Ricans do shuttle back and forth frequently between the island and New York, many others are settled on a relatively permanent basis in the city. To achieve decent lives in Hunts Point and other sections of New York, Father Fitzpatrick says they must adopt a new militancy "about their interests in antipoverty programs, education, public welfare, and housing," and about their activities "in the political arena." He foresees that this will happen.

And there are indications he is correct. In recent months, there have been various attempts to weld a new political force composed of Spanish-speaking Americans. In October, 1971, for example, Hispanic-Americans from all sections of the country met at a hotel just outside Washington, D.C., to form a political coalition. Although only about 150 persons had been expected to attend, more than 1,100 showed up. They represented Puerto Rican, Mexican-American, and other Spanish-origin groups that had formerly gone their own ways. The keynote speech was delivered by United States Senator Joseph M. Montoya of New Mexico, who began with the words "Ya basta!" (Enough is enough!). The participants in the conference range from members of Congress and state and local officials of Spanish origin to officers of about one hundred Puerto Rican and Mexican-American organizations, a handful of Cubans from Florida, a middle-aged Puerto Rican woman from Hunts Point, and a young Chicano from Tres Piedras, New Mexico.

As might have been predicted, the conference was marked by frequent disputes among representatives of various groups and among militant and moderate factions. The disputes became so bitter that Representative Badillo, who had been one of the four Spanish-speaking members of Congress to issue the original call for the meeting, stalked out—calling the conference a disaster and saying he would have nothing further to do with the coalition. Badillo was particularly insensed because the coalition voted to support the movement for Puerto Rican independence and to study the possibility of a separate Spanish-speaking political party. He felt the question of Puerto Rican independence was best left to those living on the island, and that the coalition's best chances for success rested in working within the framework of existing American political parties.

Despite Badillo's withdrawal and the intensity of the disagreements, others who attended the conference hailed the formation of the coalition as a major step in achieving the stated goal of *"unidos"* (unity). They pointed out that the conference had voted to organize a national political action campaign, to establish a permanent Washington headquarters to press for legislation and to create the machinery to act as a watchdog against repressive law-enforcement tactics aimed at Hispanic-Americans.

A month after the meeting outside Washington, a separate group with similar aims met in Pueblo, Colorado. The group, composed of about four hundred Puerto Rican and Mexican-American activists, pledged to work for a national political movement independent of the existing political parties.

Obviously, it is one thing for groups of this kind to try to organize on a national basis, and it is quite another for their activities to produce beneficial results on the local level in areas such as Hunts Point. But it seems clear that the broadest possible base of support will be necessary to give Spanish-speaking Americans the political influence they need if they are to achieve their aims. If one or more such organizations succeed in gaining political power at the national level, it is logical to assume that they will establish branches in Hunts Point and other ghetto areas populated largely by Hispanic-Americans. These local branches should, in turn, be able to exert strong influence on local and state officials. (It goes without saying that, to have maximum influence, they must also be able to work with other ethnic groups—such as Negroes and whites—within their communities.)

Assuming that such a power bloc could be established and make its presence felt on the local, state, and national levels, what sort of reforms could it bring about in Hunts Point? There are myriad ways in which it could prove effective in persuading the power structure to give the neighborhood the help it needs if it is to be reborn as a vital, viable community. The Model Cities program is an apt example. The program, launched during the administration of former President Lyndon B. Johnson, was designed to show how blighted neighborhoods could be renewed through coordinated use of federal, state, city, and private programs. If ever there were a neighborhood that could have served as a model because it most seriously needed rehabilitation, that neighborhood was Hunts Point. Yet, as previously described, Hunts Point has received only minimal aid under the Model Cities program. For one thing, only part of Hunts Point is covered by the program. For another, the aid provided thus far—while obviously welcome—has not gone to the heart of the neighborhood's problems. There has been, for example, no use of Model Cities funds to provide improved housing for the area. While other neighborhoods in New York City, and indeed, even in the Bronx, have been given new low-income housing projects under the program, the worst slum of all has been ignored. It is reasonable to assume that, if an effective political coalition could be put together in Hunts Point, it would be successful in pressing government officials to place at least one and perhaps more such projects in Hunts Point.

New housing, plus rehabilitation of existing housing, is essential if Hunts Point is to be saved. For decent housing is the *sine qua non* of urban revitalization. As the President's Committee on Urban Housing put it: "The place a man lives is more than just another commodity. It is a symbol of his status, an extension of his personality, a part of his identity, a determinant of many of the benefits—and disadvantages—of society that will come to him and his family: schooling, po-

[201]

lice protection, municipal services, neighborhood environment, access (or lack of access) to a hundred possibilities of life and culture."

If Model Cities housing were to be built in Hunts Point, what might it cost? The current estimate is that the average apartment would cost at least $30,000 to construct. A housing project built recently under the Model Cities program elsewhere in the Bronx, containing 309 apartments, cost $10,300,000. Under present regulations imposed by the United States Department of Housing and Urban Development, it would be impossible to build a project in Hunts Point solely with Model Cities Funds. The government regulations provide that no more than $27,000 in federal housing funds can be spent for each apartment constructed under the Model Cities program. Since the cost is estimated to be at least $30,000 for each apartment that might be built in Hunts Point, the difference would have to be paid from other funds, or the regulations would have to be changed.

Again, a coalition of Hispanic-Americans—working with other pressure groups—might be instrumental in forcing the government to raise the ceiling from $27,000. Proponents of increased public housing in urban ghettos argue that the $27,000 restriction, while perhaps workable in other cities, imposes undue hardships on a city with the high labor and construction costs of New York. "It is beyond us why the federal government keeps unrealistic cost limitations despite rising costs of construction," says Victor Marrero, director of one of the Model Cities programs in New York.

One advantage Hunts Point would have over other urban ghettos if one or more Model Cities projects were built there would be that there would not necessarily have to be massive relocation of current residents during the construction period. There is ample vacant land in the neighborhood to accommodate new housing without tearing down existing buildings. Once the new project or projects were built, residents of the dilapidated tenements in the area could be given priority as prospective tenants. The tenements could then be torn down and new buildings could rise on the sites.

Housing experts say many existing buildings in Hunts Point could be salvaged through extensive renovation programs. One executive of a construction firm that does substantial amounts of rehabilitation work in urban ghettos says: "I've looked at a lot of those dilapidated tenements in Hunts Point. The interiors are a mess, but the exteriors are still in good condition. We could go into those buildings, tear out the entire interiors, build new interiors, install elevators, sandblast the exteriors, and give these people an essentially new building within eight months. We could do it for about $17,000 per apartment, which is about half what it would cost for an apartment in a building that was built from scratch. We've done it elsewhere and it's worked out very well."

The executive says much of his company's work of this kind has been done under New York's municipal loan program. As previously described, this program involves loans by the city to owners of slum buildings in need of renovation. Because of the scandal that arose in the program, the city temporarily placed a moratorium on further loans. "Our company wasn't involved in the scandal," the executive says. But as a result of the moratorium, his company and other innocent firms were prevented from performing much additional work that was badly needed. Buildings in Hunts Point were among those that were neglected in the aftermath of the scandal. With proper safeguards against further abuses, the municipal loan program could provide an effective vehicle for major rehabilitation work in Hunts Point.

Of course, tenants of buildings whose interiors were to be completely replaced in a renovation campaign would have to be relocated during the construction period. But the construction executive said that would not be a formidable obstacle. "We've worked out a 'piggyback' system to avoid relocation problems," he says. "There are always some buildings in these slums that are in such bad shape that they're completely abandoned and just boarded up. We go into these buildings first, since they're vacant, and completely rebuild them—except for the exteriors. Then, when we're ready to start work on an occupied building, the tenants can move into the previously vacant buildings. From there on, it's just a 'piggyback' arrangement; as one building is finished and work starts on another, the tenants move from one building to another. But there's no major relocation problem; nobody is forced to move into another neighborhood or thrown out on the street. And if a family wants to move back into its old building after the renovation is finished, it gets first crack at the apartments."

The New York City Planning Commission, in a voluminous report on problems existing in the Bronx, has emphasized the urgent need for improved housing in Hunts Point. Commission officials said that the Bronx "needs more help and needs it faster than any other borough of the city." And by far the most serious problem in the Bronx, they said, was the deterioration in Hunts Point and adjacent neighborhoods.

The commission report described conditions in the area in these terms: "Bleak tenements line block after block. The teeming district is peppered with shabby warehouses, lofts, garages, marginal businesses, and trash-strewn lots. Schools are extremely overcrowded, and green space is all but nonexistent. The welfare load is twice the city average. The district is more crime-ridden than any other. Rapid social change in recent years has left few stable social or political organizations."

Donald H. Elliott, the commission chairman, said these conditions posed the most serious problems in the city. "But it is not impossible to solve them," he said. "It is going to take a lot of work and a lot of money." The trouble is that the planning commission's recognition of the seriousness of the situation is no guarantee that "a lot of work and a lot of money" is going to be expended on a solution. The commission has proposed ambitious steps for coping with the area's decay—including major housing construction projects—but it has not reduced these suggestions to specifics. And to date, no concrete measures have been taken to implement the proposals.

A chief stumbling block in the way of improved housing conditions for Hunts Point is the Lindsay administration's commitment to a theory known as "scattered-site" low-income housing. The theory is that, instead of building new low-income housing projects in slums, the forces of government and private enterprise should scatter such developments throughout the city's middle-income neighborhoods. That way, it is argued, poor people will be able to move out of the slums and reap the benefits of life in neighborhoods with better conditions.

Such strategy was advocated by the National Advisory Commission on Civil Disorders, of which Mayor Lindsay was vice-chairman. The commission, after investigating the urban riots of 1967, warned: "Our nation is moving toward two societies, one black, one white—separate and unequal. . . . To date, housing programs serving low-income groups have been concentrated in the ghettos. We believe that federally aided low- and moderate-income housing programs must be reoriented so that the major thrust is in non-ghetto areas. . . . If this is not done, those programs will continue to concentrate the most impoverished and dependent segments of the population into the central-city ghettos, where there is already a critical gap between the needs of the population and the public resources to deal with them. This can only continue to compound the conditions of failure and hopelessness which lead to crime, civil disorder, and social disorganization."

The "scattered-site" theory springs from the most compassionate of motives and sounds fine on paper. But the fact is that it has been virtually impossible to implement, particularly in New York City, because residents of middle-income neighborhoods are violently opposed to accepting low-income projects designed to draw people away from the ghettos. The most recent example of such opposition arose in the Forest Hills section of Queens, a largely white, middle-class section of the city. An 840-unit low-income housing project was planned there by the city. The antagonism of local residents toward the project boiled over into angry confrontations, including attempts by some of the residents to set fire to a construction company's temporary headquarters on the project site. At this writing, the city insists it will go through with its construction plans, but the residents are trying to halt the project through court action. Even if the city wins the fight, the prospects for harmonious relations between current residents and the newcomers who would enter the project seem dim.

Because of opposition such as that voiced by Forest Hills residents, the "scattered-site" program has been an abysmal failure in New York thus far. Since the Lindsay administration took office on January 1, 1966, the city has begun construction on 16,732 low-income apartments. Of those, only 2,647 have been outside the slums. And not one has been in Hunts Point.

The "scattered-site" program, even if successful, would fail to reckon with Hunts Point's special problems. Assuming that large numbers of Hunts Pointers could be relocated into new housing projects in other sections of the city—and that is a big assumption—what about the housing they would leave behind? It would still be in perhaps the worst condition of any housing in the city. Even though it remained unrehabilitated, there is every reason to believe that new immigrants to New York—particularly from Puerto Rico—would move into it because it would be the least expensive housing available. Thus one group of slum-dwellers would be replaced by another, and the cycle of deterioration would continue unabated.

It seems likely that a high-pressure campaign will have to be waged to persuade city, state, and federal officials to commit the funds, time, and energy necessary to bring decent housing to Hunts Point. Still again, a political coalition would provide the means of conducting such a campaign. Unless the housing situation is markedly improved, there can be little hope for achieving other reforms in Hunts Point.

But, assuming the housing problems could be solved or at least substantially alleviated, what could be done about the broad spectrum of other afflictions that plague Hunts Point? For example, what could be done about drug addiction and related crime?

There seems little question that current programs for combating Hunts Point's burgeoning addiction problem are inadequate. Such programs as the one conducted by SERA (described in Chapter Ten) seem to be producing beneficial results, but are reaching only a fraction of Hunts Point's addict population. SERA, for instance, handles only about two hundred addicts at a time. There is no precise knowledge about the number of addicts in Hunts Point, but the best estimate is that one out of five residents uses heroin. If that estimate is accurate, there are more than 32,000 heroin users in the neighborhood. Even allowing for the fact that the estimate may be high and that all users are not addicts, that is still an enormous number.

To give some idea of the size of Hunts Point's drug problem and the inadequacy of efforts to cope with it, one need only note that Mayor Lindsay's Narcotics Control Council recently announced a major expansion of its citywide metha-done maintenance program—increasing the number of per-sons to be treated from 3,000 to 11,000. In other words, the city's entire program for providing methadone—even under the expansion—would be capable of handling only about a third of Hunts Point's heroin users if no patients were ac-cepted from any other sections of New York. Obviously, the city could not pour its entire budget for methadone treat-ment into Hunts Point alone. But, even if it did, the program would not begin to meet the area's needs.

The city itself recognizes the inadequacy of the program. It estimates there are about 125,000 addicts in New York, yet allocates enough money to treat only 11,000. That al-location totals $12,500,000 a year. Thus, it can be assumed that, if a methadone program could be devised and funded to treat every heroin user in Hunts Point, it would cost some-where in the neighborhood of $37,500,000 a year. Such amounts would not have to be spent indefinitely, however, since methadone programs are intended to wean patients off all drugs—including methadone—over the long haul. To be sure, a program costing $37,500,000 sounds staggering. But is the price tag so enormous that such a program is not worth considering, even if it might sharply reduce a crime problem that is taking millions of dollars' worth of stolen goods from Hunts Pointers every year and inflicting count-less violent deaths and injuries?

Some experts say it is not too high a price to pay if it can substantially curb the heroin traffic in the neighborhood. They concede, however, that the chances of such large amounts ever being allocated for a methadone program in Hunts Point are negligible. Others familiar with the problem favor a program that would rely not on methadone but on simply providing addicts with free, legalized injections of heroin—thus removing the necessity for them to steal in order to support their habits. Although such a system was tried in England and was not considered successful, its advocates believe it might work in New York.

Among these advocates is Hunts Point's representative in the New York State Senate, Robert Garcia. "The people in my district have had it," Senator Garcia says. "Junkies are robbing them in broad daylight. We need some action and we need it now. We ought to give them [the addicts] the drugs." He concedes that he is uncertain how such a program could be administered.

But another proponent of the idea has worked out a fundamental plan for putting such a system into operation. This proponent, New York City Criminal Court Judge Robert S. Kriendler, describes the plan in these terms: "A system should be created under a state commission to provide heroin for these addicts. Around-the-clock storefront centers should be opened in various parts of the city where anyone who wishes a shot of heroin could get a fix free of charge. Such addicts would be provided with an identification card with a photograph and a serial number, so that such treatment would be confined only to those needing it." Judge Kriendler, who spent many years as a federal prosecutor before going on the bench, says such a program would "drive all the illegal drug pushers out of business." Once the pushers were eliminated, he says, there would be nobody available to lure young people onto drugs. Since the illicit supply of drugs presumably would be dried up and the storefront centers would provide heroin only to those already addicted, Judge Kriendler foresees an eventual phasing out of addiction. All of this, of course, presupposes that federal as well as state legislation would authorize the establishment of the heroin-supply centers. For, no matter what legislation a state passes, existing federal law makes it a crime to possess or transfer heroin, and this law would apply to state-operated facilities as well as to illicit private traffickers. If federal and state approval could be obtained and such a program could be put into effect, Judge Kriendler estimates that as much as seventy-five percent of all crime in ghettos such as Hunts Point could be eliminated.

While debate may rage over the best means of doing the job, there can be no disputing the contention that *something* must be done to curb the alarming rate of heroin addiction in Hunts Point. To allow the current addiction and resulting crime rampage to continue unabated would be nothing short of criminal itself. More effective law enforcement can help, but it is clear that police activity alone cannot solve a problem of this magnitude. If the nation received word tomorrow that a cholera epidemic was about to strike a neighborhood such as Hunts Point and infect as many as 32,000 persons, it is unquestionable that the country would somehow find the resources to combat the disease. Is an epidemic of narcotics addiction of comparable proportions to be greeted only by public indifference outside the immediate area affected? If so, this country is in greater trouble than even the most pessimistic Jeremiahs contend.

Assuming that some means can be found to limit substantially the number of addicts in Hunts Point, there would still be a serious crime problem in the area. Part of that problem would be ameliorated if the housing improvements discussed earlier in this chapter were effected. New housing projects, for example, could be expected to provide tenants tighter security than the current tenements. While security in such projects is not always easy to provide, as has become evident in high-rise developments built in other sections of New York and elsewhere, it is nonetheless more readily obtainable than in the present chaotic housing in Hunts Point. Intercom systems permitting tenants to question visitors outside the lobby doors before pushing buzzers to allow them entry could be installed. Guards or doormen could be stationed in the lobbies of high-rise buildings at far less expense than would be necessary to station such men in the various smaller tenements throughout the neighborhood. In addition, if the projects were under the jurisdiction of the City Housing Authority, they would be protected by members of the authority's police force.

Beyond all that, there is an obvious need for improved protection from the city police department. The 41st Precinct urgently needs substantial manpower additions. There must also be increased attention paid to Hunts Point by specialized units within the department, such as the narcotics bureau. But law enforcement, as policemen constantly point out, depends on other elements besides police departments. The court system in the Bronx, as in other areas, is in drastic need of overhaul. It is loaded down with a backlog of cases, is inefficient, and often acts as a mere revolving door. Officers in the 41st Precinct recite case after case in which they have arrested persons in the act of committing crimes, only to see them back on the streets of Hunts Point within hours. Suspects often are arrested as many as a half-dozen times and released on bail each time while the cases against them lie stagnant in the courts. When they finally do come to trial, policemen say, judges frequently let them off with suspended sentences or short jail terms that return them to the streets to commit still more crimes.

As with other reforms needed in Hunts Point, the curbing of crime will take money—money for more policemen, for more equipment, for improved courts, and the like. Where such money might be obtained is an open question. One seemingly logical answer would be the federal government, since President Nixon's administration won power largely on its promises to provide the country with "law and order." But recent actions of the administration make such aid for Hunts Point appear unlikely. The administration has revealed plans to launch a $160 million campaign to cut burglary and street crime in major cities with high crime rates. The plans, however, apply only to cities with populations between 250,000 and 1,000,000. That would eliminate New York and its ghettos, including Hunts Point. The ostensible reason for omitting the cites with 1,000,000 or more residents was that there would not be sufficient funds available to have a measurable impact there. But this reasoning leaves something to be desired. The very cities that have the most serious crime problems are the ones that have been left out of the program. Even if there were limited funds, critics charge, it would have made more sense to use them in areas of most urgent need—instead of dispensing them to cities whose populations and problems were both smaller. Again, here is a case where an effective political organization lobbying on behalf of ghetto residents might have made an important contribution by putting the heat on the administration to reorder its priorities.

Another major area in which Hunts Point needs urgent help is in business and job development. If the neighborhood is to be reclaimed, thousands of its unemployed residents must be given jobs and its dying businesses must be given new leases on life. An important first step has been taken toward alleviating the depressed economic conditions. In September, 1971, the United States Department of Commerce designated Hunts Point as a special redevelopment area—thus opening the door to the possible granting of millions of dollars in federal aid for job development, industrial expansion, technical assistance, and commercial development. Commerce Department officials say special emphasis will be placed on developing minority-owned businesses in the neighborhood. In addition, they say, the federal government will put up funds to pay for the relocation of large industries that agree to move into Hunts Point. The government will also help finance the expansion of existing businesses in the neighborhood and will provide aid to developers who agree to build industrial parks there.

It is too early to tell how successful this program will be.

At this point, no federal funds have actually been spent. There will have to be continuing pressure, not only on government officials but also on private corporations, to assure that the program is implemented. But it does seem that this program represents one of the most hopeful signs in Hunts Point's recent history.

If it succeeds, it should go a long way toward relieving another Hunts Point problem—the large percentage of families on welfare. In Hunts Point, as elsewhere, there are some slothful welfare recipients. But for every one of these there are many more who sincerely want to work their way off the welfare rolls. To do so, they need jobs—jobs that have long been unavailable in Hunts Point and even in other areas of the city. The economic revitalization of Hunts Point could take thousands of men, women, and teen-agers away from the ranks of public charges and place them on the road to more productive, meaningful lives.

All of this—improved housing, reduction of drug addiction and related crime, economic development, increased employment, decreased dependence on welfare assistance, and countless other benefits—can be obtained. It is within reach—a long reach, perhaps, but not an impossible one. Yes, it will take enormous amounts of money. Yes, it will take time and energy and vision. But it can be achieved.

No matter what its fate, Hunts Point offers a multitude of lessons for numerous other communities throughout the United States. It demonstrates that no urban neighborhood —no matter how stable its population has been, no matter how rich its history, no matter how comfortable its homes— is safe from the hazards of rapid, sickening deterioration. It demonstrates what can happen when white residents panic and flee because "they" are threatening to move into the neighborhood. It demonstrates the disastrous consequences of public indifference toward the myriad of problems that confront the nation's poor, dark-skinned citizens. It demonstrates the absurdity of the reasoning that what happens in the ghetto is of little importance to other sections of a megalopolis. It demonstrates that urban deterioration does not level off and halt of its own accord; its roots continue to sink ever deeper unless drastic action is taken to curb it. And it demonstrates that, the longer society waits to address itself to remedying the ills of urban decay, the greater will be the cost in dollars, lives, and human misery.

What has happened in Hunts Point is not markedly different from what has happened in Harlem, Bedford-Stuyvesant, Watts, Hough, and the slums of Newark, Detroit, and other American cities. What is different about Hunts Point is that the deterioration occurred there much more quickly and completely than elsewhere. It not only became perhaps the nation's worst ghetto—its conversion took place in less than half the time that it took in most other slums.

Of course, that is all the more reason why the rebirth of Hunts Point could serve as a symbol of American determination to reclaim its dying neighborhoods. If Hunts Point can be saved, there is no ghetto that is beyond redemption.

During the period of Hunts Point's greatest deterioration, the United States has had three Presidents, John F. Kennedy, Lyndon B. Johnson, and Richard M. Nixon. All have spoken movingly of the urgent need to improve the lot of America's poor, downtrodden minority groups.

President Kennedy said: "It ought to be possible for every American to enjoy the privileges of being American without regard to his race or his color. In short, every American ought to have the right to be treated as he would wish to be treated, as one would wish his children to be treated. But this is not the case. The Negro baby born in America today, regardless of the section of the nation in which he is born, has about one half as much chance of completing high school as a white baby born in the same place on the same day, one third as much chance of completing college, one third as much chance of becoming a professional man, twice as much chance of becoming unemployed, about one-seventh as much chance of earning $10,000 a year, a life expectancy which is seven years shorter, and the prospects of earning only half as much. . . . If an American, because his skin is dark, cannot . . . enjoy the full and free life which all of us want, then who among us would be content to have the color of his skin changed and stand in his place? Who among us would then be content with the counsels of patience and delay?"

President Johnson said: "The only genuine, long-range solution [to urban decay] lies in an attack—mounted at every level—upon the conditions that breed despair and violence. All of us know what those conditions are: ignorance, discrimination, slums, poverty, disease, not enough jobs. We should attack these conditions—not because we are frightened by conflict, but because we are fired by conscience. We should attack them because there is simply no other way to achieve a decent and orderly society in America."

President Nixon said: "We shall build a better America in which we shall see the realization of the dreams of millions of people for a fuller, richer life than men have ever known in the history of mankind. . . . I believe in the American dream because I have seen it come true in my own life."

Each of these Presidents, to a varying degree, has matched his rhetoric with action. Yet the ghettos remain. The time has come, at last, when this nation must move dramatically to turn the tide of urban deterioration. To do otherwise would be to declare moral bankruptcy. And there is no more symbolic place to begin than in Hunts Point.

ACKNOWLEDGMENTS

I am deeply indebted to the people of Hunts Point, past and present, for their generous help in the preparation of this book. Almost without exception, they have been unfailingly receptive to the spirit in which the project was undertaken. They have welcomed me into their homes, opened their hearts, and in some cases bared their souls—from the prostitutes and junkies to the policemen, and from the welfare mothers to the old-time residents who now live in affluent suburbs. Regrettably, many public officials whose help I sought in researching the book did not react with comparable zeal. They evidently felt the political risks were too great for them to cooperate with an author writing about a potential "hot potato" such as Hunts Point. To those few officials who did agree to help, I would like to express my gratitude and my admiration for their courage.

To those in the publishing world who played roles in preparation of the book—especially Elizabeth Otis, Richard Kennedy, and Ross Claiborne—my thanks for faith, counsel, and uncommon amounts of patience.

To a writer friend, Joan Doviak, my thanks for helping me research several angles of the Hunts Point story in Washington, D.C.

Once again, I am indebted to my wife, Jeanne, and my daughters, Pamela and Patricia, for their willingness to put up with life in a writer's household. I am particularly grateful for their forebearance during the period when I was conducting research in the Hunts Point "jungle." Despite fears for my safety, they were unstintingly enthusiastic about the necessity for writing this book.